Clear Speech
Student's Book

Clear Speech

Pronunciation and Listening Comprehension in American English

Student's Book

Judy B. Gilbert

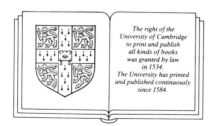

The right of the
University of Cambridge
to print and publish
all kinds of books
was granted by law
in 1534.
The University has printed
and published continuously
since 1584.

Cambridge University Press

Cambridge

London   New York   New Rochelle

Melbourne   Sydney

Published by the Press Syndicate of the University of Cambridge
The Pitt Building, Trumpington Street, Cambridge CB2 1RP
32 East 57th Street, New York, NY 10022, USA
10 Stamford Road, Oakleigh, Melbourne 3166, Australia

© Cambridge University Press 1984

First published 1984
Fourth printing 1987

Printed in the United States of America

Library of Congress Cataloging in Publication Data
Gilbert, Judy B. (Judy Bogen)
Clear speech.
Bibliography: p.
1. English language – Study and teaching – Foreign
speakers. 2. English language – United States –
Pronunciation. I. Title.
PE1128.A2G5 1984 428.3′4 83-15416

ISBN 0 521 28790 1 (Student's Book)
ISBN 0 521 28791 X (Teacher's Manual)
ISBN 0 521 24570 2 (Cassette)

Dedicated to the memory of my mother,
Esther Bogen Tietz, M.D.

Contents

LISTENING

CLEAR SPEECH

Acknowledgments

Many people helped with this book. First, I would like to thank two people whose encouragement was especially important to me:

Virginia French Allen, for her profoundly practical advice and for her sensitivity toward both student and teacher.

Dwight L. Bolinger, for his generous patience in explaining linguistic theory, and also for serving as a model of what a scholar should be.

Also thanks to Joseph Bogen, M.D., for fixing my attention on science; J. Donald Bowen, for teaching the importance of contextualizing pronunciation practice; Gillian Brown, for the clarity of her writing on intonation; Stephen Krashen, for his encouragement and theoretical insights; Joan Morley, for leading the way in teaching listening comprehension; John Ohala, for his severe standards for science; Dorothy Overly, for her inspiring teaching; and my teaching partners, for their personal support and sharing of ideas for so many years: Beryl Duffin, Rebecca Ford, Beth Greenwood, Julia Hunter-Blair, and Tippy Schwabe.

Thanks to the twenty-five teachers who field tested this book at twelve institutions in five countries. Their contributions were immensely helpful in making the book more teachable, and I gratefully list their names in the Teacher's Manual.

Thanks to A. R. Evans, for being such an able author's agent.

Thanks to Christine Cairns, Sandra Graham, Adrian du Plessis, and Ellen Shaw of Cambridge University Press, for their thorough and clear-sighted editing.

Thanks especially to my family: my father, J. B. Tietz, for teaching me to value exact language; my daughters, Vicky, Jeane, and Tania, for growing up to be good people. And last, because he is first, thanks to my husband, Jerry.

Judy B. Gilbert

Cover design by Frederick Charles Ltd.
Book design by Peter Ducker

Cassette production by The Sun Group. The recording of "The Entertainer" played by Max Morath courtesy of Vanguard Recording Society, Inc., New York, New York.

Foreword

The many real-life embodiments of the student from abroad who reads the *New York Times* but cannot utter an intelligible word in English are a measure of our failure to teach the paramount skill of putting words into mouths rather than on pages of print. Why has something so obviously necessary been so little concentrated upon?

In part it must be because how to speak and listen correctly is seen as too technical – a subject that involves phonetics and phonemes and phonology and all that, something too abstract and abstruse for teachers to master, and certainly far over the heads of students. Better to play it safe, serve the best you can as a model of correct English, and trust to luck that your students will get the hang of it.

Judy Gilbert's book, *Clear Speech*, proves that it is no longer necessary for pronunciation and listening comprehension to be the stepsisters of grammar and vocabulary, those other regions of English that we have always been bold enough not only to model in the classroom but to talk about in more or less technical terms. She has measured the technical needs, selected what is required to meet them from the scientific descriptions of English pronunciation, and put the explanations in nontechnical terms. To these carefully and sparingly defined principles she has added sharply delineated examples and exercises and woven the whole together with a high degree of art.

Here is a book that brings information about how English is spoken within the grasp of learners for whom it is vital to understanding and being understood in American society. It is a book that makes pronunciation teachable, and the learning of it as pleasant as any serious learning can be.

Dwight Bolinger

Palo Alto, California

To the student

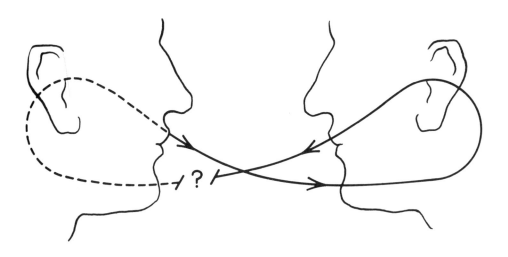

Conversation flow

When you are speaking in a new language, sometimes the other person may not understand. The other person may say "What?" or may misunderstand your ideas. Worse yet, the other person may get embarrassed and stop the conversation. Each of these instances is a *break in communication*, small or large. It is like a break in the flow (or movement) of electricity in an electrical circuit. If the flow is stopped at any place in the circuit, the whole system stops. When something blocks the flow of ideas, the conversation stops.

You need to know how to analyze these breaks in communication. If you can find the problem quickly, you can correct it quickly. Then the conversation can flow again. Some breaks in communication are caused by vocabulary or grammar mistakes. Other breaks are caused by mistakes in pronunciation. It is not necessary to pronounce each sound perfectly in order to be understood. Only a few parts of each sentence are really important, but these few parts are essential. The native speaker depends on hearing these parts clearly. Therefore, you need to know which parts of a sentence must be clear, and how to make them clear.

Foreign students planning to attend American universities see the TOEFL examination as a door to their studies: Will it be open or closed? What skills are most important for achieving a high enough score? What is the most efficient way to prepare for the examination? Even more important, what is the most effective preparation for work in an American university?

Extensive research indicates that any practice that can help you comprehend meaning in English will help you both in the test and in university work. Improvement in listening comprehension is the most important guarantee of a relatively easy and efficient experience in the university. As one student commented, after two years of graduate study in the United States, "Our difficulties are in inverse proportion to our strength in English."

This book concentrates on the ways that English pronunciation helps the listener understand the meaning. The book begins with a short test designed to help you know how clearly you can hear spoken English.

Symbols used in the text

Slashes identify reduced vowels.

> Example: bánaná

Parentheses signal reduction of the letter "h."

> Example: Is (h)e busy? (sounds like "Izzybizzy?")

Rising and falling lines indicate the pitch of words and sentences.

> Example: eleven   Is she there?

Bars and dots identify long and short syllables.

> Example: record (noun)   record (verb)

Capital letters indicate stress.

> Example: I WANT a baNAna.

Cassette tape

marks sections that are recorded on the cassette tape.

Name ————————————————————   Date ——————————

Country ————————————————————

Clear Listening Test 🔲

The purpose of this test is to find what parts of English pronunciation may interfere with the way you understand and use spoken English. How you *hear* English is closely connected with how you *speak* English.

This test is recorded on the Cassette.

Part 1: Stressed syllables (10 points)

Draw a line under the most stressed syllable. Mark only *one* syllable for each word. Examples:

a. de<u>lay</u>
b. <u>bro</u>ken
c. edu<u>ca</u>tion

   Now listen and draw a line under the most stressed syllable. You will hear each word twice.

1. participating   3. photography   5. university
2. photograph   4. alternative

Part 2: Vowel clarity (10 points)

Draw a line through the unclear (not clearly pronounced) vowels in each word. Examples:

a. áround
b. atóm
c. átomíc

   Now listen to the following words and draw a line through the unclear vowels. You will hear each word twice.

1. banana   3. woman   5. America
2. Nebraska   4. women

Part 3: Voicing and length of syllable (10 points)

You will hear one sentence from each of the following pairs of sentences. That sentence will be read twice. Put a check next to the sentence you hear.

1a. What kind of word is "use"?   (noun)   —
 b. What kind of word is "use"?   (verb)   —
2a. He said "prove."   (verb)   —
 b. He said "proof."   (noun)   —
3a. What does "loose" mean?   (adjective)   —
 b. What does "lose" mean?   (verb)   —
4a. What kind of cap was it?   —
 b. What kind of cab was it?   —

5a. What's the prize? —
 b. What's the price? —

Part 4: Pitch patterns – words (10 points)

You will hear some American names. Draw a pitch pattern for each name. Examples:

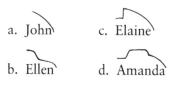

a. John   c. Elaine

b. Ellen   d. Amanda

Now listen and draw the pitch patterns. You will hear each name twice.

1. Barbara   3. Jonathan   5. Victor

2. Corinne   4. Elizabeth

Part 5: Pitch patterns – sentences (10 points)

You will hear some sentences. Draw a pitch line for the sentence. Examples:

a. Where did you go?

b. Is she there?

Now listen to these sentences and draw the pitch pattern. You will hear each sentence twice.

1. It was awful!

2. She left her book.

3. She left her book?

4. This is my notebook. (not my textbook)

5. This is my notebook. (not yours)

Part 6: Contractions, reductions (20 points)

You will hear some sentences. Write the missing words. Examples:

a. She __*can't*__ go.
b. He __*isn't*__ going.

   Now listen to the sentences and write the missing words. You will hear each sentence *once*.

1. She doesn't _____ study now.

2. Please _____ the information.

3. _____ think she'll win?

4. Where _____ go?

5. How _____ you been here?

6. _____ busy?

7. Where _____ store?

8. Did _____ to the concert?

9. What _____ done?

10. Is _____ good?

Part 7: Focus words (20 points)

You will hear a dialogue. Underline the one most emphasized word in each sentence. You will hear the dialogue only once. Example:

A: That's a <u>great</u> idea!

A: What's the matter?
B: I lost my hat.
A: What kind of hat?
B: It was a rain hat.
A: What color rain hat?
B: It was white. White with stripes.
A: There was a white hat with stripes in the car.
B: Which car?
A: The one I sold.

Part 8: Thought groups (10 points)

Intonation helps the listener recognize groups of words. To test your awareness of the intonation markers for thought groups, you will hear one of a pair of sentences. Put a check (√) next to the sentence you hear. Example:

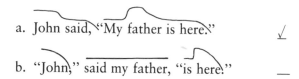

a. John said, "My father is here."   √

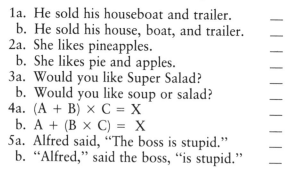

b. "John," said my father, "is here."   —

   Now listen to one sentence from each of the following pairs of sentences. Put a check next to the sentence you hear. You will hear each sentence twice.

1a. He sold his houseboat and trailer.   —
 b. He sold his house, boat, and trailer.   —
2a. She likes pineapples.   —
 b. She likes pie and apples.   —
3a. Would you like Super Salad?   —
 b. Would you like soup or salad?   —
4a. $(A + B) \times C = X$ —
 b. $A + (B \times C) = X$ —
5a. Alfred said, "The boss is stupid."   —
 b. "Alfred," said the boss, "is stupid."   —

SYLLABLE UNITS

1 · Syllables

The syllable is the basic unit of English pronunciation.  Listen to the following words and notice how some of them have two or more parts.

1 syllable	2 syllables	3 syllables
ease	easy	easily
will	willing	willingly

As you listen to the following words, tap your hand on the desk to help count each syllable.

1	2	3	4
one	seven	eleven	identify
two	eighteen	direction	analysis
down	sentence	syllable	He wants a book.
step	working	important	We were happy.
stress	focus	emphasis	It's important.

Now read the same list aloud, tapping syllables while you speak.

B

Say your name out loud, and decide how many syllables there are in it. See if the other members of the class agree. Do not worry if the class cannot agree on every name, especially where two vowels come together. You only need to have a rough sense of the number of syllables.

C

Practice saying these words, tapping the syllables. Be careful not to add or subtract syllables. Decide how many syllables there are in the words in the third column.

1	2	3 *or more*
write	writer	academic
round	rounder	sentences
fish	fishy	registration
wind	windy	international
blow	below	classification
prayed	parade	economy
school	student	economical

D

Grammar mistakes are often the result of a failure to recognize the number of syllables. Examples:

> a. They have rent (rented) an apartment.
> b. There are two dish (dishes).

Listen to the following words. Which words have one syllable and which have two syllables?

painted	rented	added	caused
crowded	worked	faded	filled
walked	laughed	watched	closed

Rule: Regular past tense verbs that end in a "d" or "t" sound in the basic form will add an extra syllable in the past tense. Look over the list above and see how this rule works.

E

Answer the following questions aloud, using the verb in the past. Be careful of the final syllable. Example:

> Q: Did you rent an apartment yet?
> A: Yes, I rented one yesterday.

1. When did you rent your apartment?
2. Did you walk here today?
3. When did you start studying English?
4. Did you use an English dictionary this morning?
5. What did your country export last year? or import? (If you do not know, guess.)
6. Did you travel far this year?
7. Did you watch TV last night?
8. Did you request a visa to any country this year?
9. Did you listen to the radio last night?
10. What did you intend to do today?

F

Some words end in sounds called *sibilants*. A sibilant is a sound like "s."
Sibilants have a hissing noise, like a snake. Examples:

hi<u>ss</u>, bu<u>zz</u>, fi<u>sh</u>, <u>ch</u>ur<u>ch</u>, <u>j</u>u<u>dg</u>e, bo<u>x</u>

**Rule: Nouns and verbs ending in a sibilant in their basic form have an extra
syllable when an "s" is added.**

Listen and then practice saying these pairs.

Noun + plural ending	*Verb + 3rd person singular*
rose....roses	wash......washes
kiss ....kisses	cause......causes
dish....dishes	advise.....advises
watch..watches	change....changes
judge...judges	mix.......mixes
box.....boxes	surprise...surprises

Listen to your teacher or another student say one word from each of the
following pairs. Underline the word you hear.

1. /s/

lace......laces
face......faces
price.....prices
juice.....juices
excuse...excuses
fence.....fences

2. /z/

nose....noses
quiz ....quizzes
praise...praises
cheese..cheeses
size.....sizes
freeze...freezes

3. /ch/

bench....benches
lunch....lunches
speech...speeches
match ...matches
beach....beaches
roach....roaches

4. /dg/

page.....pages
edge......edges
bridge ...bridges
sponge...sponges
stage.....stages
age.......ages

5. /sh/

wish....wishes
flash ...flashes
blush...blushes
rush....rushes
crash...crashes

6. /ks/

box....boxes
sex.....sexes
six.....sixes
fix .....fixes
coax...coaxes

7. Mixed sounds

bruise....bruises
blouse...blouses
house....houses
miss......misses
teach ....teaches
choose...chooses
crunch...crunches
mess.....messes

G

Practice saying the following words. Some have an extra syllable and some do not.

Past tense	3rd person singular	Plural
completed	completes	faces
avoided	avoids	prices
smiled	smiles	mixes
caused	causes	bridges
predicted	predicts	boxes
guarded	guards	guards
mixed	mixes	quizzes
arranged	arranges	watches
washed	washes	sentences

H

Sometimes it is difficult for foreign students to hear the word "is" when it follows a sibilant sound. Listen to the following sentences. Some are complete, but some are missing a syllable. Write "right" if the sentence you hear is complete. Write "wrong" if a syllable is missing. Example:

(If you hear) "The ice cold"   *wrong*

1a. The ice is cold.   _____

b. The ice cold.   _____

2a. Her dress is pretty.   _____

b. Her dress pretty.   _____

3a. The bus late.   _____

b. The bus is late.   _____

4a. The buses are late.   _____

b. The bus are late.   _____

5a. He washes the dishes.   _____

b. He wash the dishes.   _____

6a. He need a bike.   _____

b. He needed a bike.   _____

7a. She visit her sister.   _____

b. She visited her sister.   _____

8a. The river flooded the valley.   _____

b. The river flood the valley.   _____

9a. This book was printed with ink. _____

 b. This book was print with ink. _____

10a. Yesterday we rent an apartment. _____

 b. Yesterday we rented an apartment. _____

Note: Contractions (loss of a vowel) are normal in spoken English. But the vowel cannot be contracted between two sibilants. No matter how short, this syllable is part of the rhythm of the sentence.

Contraction possible	*Contraction not possible*
I have ....I've	this is...ice is
she is.....she's	bus is...dress is
man is ...man's	
book is...book's	

I [ ] 📼

Dictation. Listen to these sentences and write the words that are missing.

1. They've already _____ the apartment for her.

2. He didn't really _____ that much money.

3. She's trying to _____ everything.

4. We've just _____ to learn irregular verbs.

5. You'll need two more _____ for all those _____ .

 Listen and write these sentences. Count the syllables you have written.

6. _____ .

7. _____ .

8. _____ .

9. _____ .

Self-analysis

Record yourself saying the following sentence several times. Then listen to the recording. Check the number of syllables very carefully. It is difficult to hear your own mistakes, but it is essential.

> This is the first city they visited when they traveled around the country, and they liked it very much.

Did you have two syllables for "this is"? Two syllables for "city"? Two syllables for "traveled"? Three syllables for "visited"? One syllable for "liked"?

WORD UNITS

2 • Stress: pitch

You need to be able to use the English stress system. Clarity in English depends on stress. English has three ways to signal stress. All three signals are used at the same time, in order to make absolutely clear which syllables are stressed. The three signals of stress are:

1. Pitch change
2. Length of vowel
3. Vowel clarity

The most powerful signal of stress is a change of pitch on the vowel.

A

Listen to the rising and falling pitch of these words. In which direction is the change of pitch?

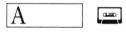 rising   one? two? three? four?

    falling   one. two. three. four.

    rising and falling   five? six. eight? nine.

B

Listen to the following words and practice saying them with a falling pitch.

1. Step-down:

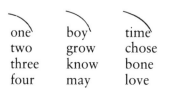

seven	twenty	fifty
record (noun)	contrast (noun)	present (noun)
sofa	painting	baby
teacher	painter	baker

2. Glide-down:

one	boy	time
two	grow	chose
three	know	bone
four	may	love

C

Listen to the following words and practice saying them with a rise-fall pitch.

1. Step-down:

eleven   important   direction
some money   his lesson   their office
I want it   He wants it.   They want it.

2. Glide-down:

alive   the boy   a pen
record (verb)   contract (verb)   object (verb)

D

Single words said alone have a falling pitch at the end. Also, most sentences end with a falling pitch.    Listen and then practice saying these words and sentences.

1. (noun)   (verb)

record ...record
object ....object
suspect ...suspect
present ...present

2a. Let's make a record of that song.   Let's record that song.
  b. What's this little object?   We object to that.
  c. That's the suspect.   They suspect him of murder.
  d. We gave her a present.   They plan to present an award.

E

Listen to these words. Underline the syllable with the highest pitch.

semester   admission
quarter   applicant
division   application
registration   education
enrollment

13

Listen to these words. Draw a pitch pattern over each word.

requirements   residence

graduate   degree

career   agricultural

graduation   professional

Compare the pronunciation of your name in your own language with the way Americans pronounce your name. Can you hear a difference in the pitch pattern? If you can analyze the American mispronunciation of your name (or any word from your language, such as the name of a city), then you can learn something useful about the rules of English. Try to imitate the American pronunciation of your name, in contrast to your own pronunciation.

Draw a pitch line for your name as you pronounce it in your own language.

Listen to the following common American names. Draw a pitch line for each name. The name that is listed first is the most formal one. Next to that is an informal form. Last comes the least formal form, which has a "-y" or "-ie" ending.

Male   *Female*

1. James, Jim, Jimmy   1. Elizabeth, Beth, Betty

2. William, Bill, Billy   2. Patricia, Pat, Patty

3. Robert, Bob, Bobby   3. Susan, Sue, Suzie

I ▭

Dictation. Listen to these sentences and write the words that are missing.

1. He's studying ————————.
2. They've decided to eat in a ————————.
3. That woman's name is ————————.
4. His name is Thomas, but everyone calls him ————————.
5. We're learning to hear American ————————.

Self-analysis

Record the following words several times. Then listen to the recording.

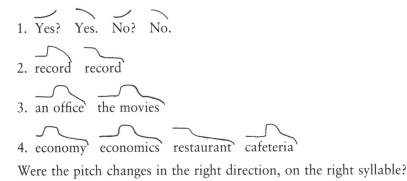

1. Yes? Yes. No? No.

2. record   record

3. an office   the movies

4. economy economics restaurant cafeteria

Were the pitch changes in the right direction, on the right syllable?

3 · Stress: length

Besides pitch change, another signal of English stress is *length*. Perhaps in your language, every syllable has the same length. That is, each syllable may take the same amount of time to say. In English, some syllables are short and some are long. Syllables are extra long when they are stressed. The extra length of the vowel gives time to hear the pitch change, showing stress.

A

Listen to this word:

> banana

Which syllable is the longest? Practice saying the word, making a careful distinction between the long syllable and the two short syllables.

Listen to these words. Notice the length of the *second* syllable:

B

The following exercise is designed to help you train yourself to hear differences in vowel length. The vowels in column 2 should be longer than the vowels in column 1.

Listen and then practice saying each word of the pair with a different length of time for the vowel. Say the words again, reversing the order (be / beat).

1	*2*		*1*	*2*
.	—		.	—
beat....be			pipe...pie	
mate ...may			rope ..row	
sight....sigh			keep ..key	
cute ....cue			soup..Sue	
boat....bow			cape ..Kay	
white...why			make..may	
date ....day			like ...lie	
			joke...Joe	
			seek ..see	

C

Listen and then practice saying the following words, concentrating on the different duration (length in time) of the syllables.

— .　　　— .　　　— .　　　. —

sofa	steaming	summer	allow
broken	easy	movies	annoy
roses	creamy	rented	around
loaded .	heated	handle	arouse

D

Listen and then practice the duration contrast in the following pairs.
Example:

Where's the rebel?　　They plan to rebel.

| Noun | Verb | | Noun | Verb | | Adjective | Verb |
| — . | . — | | . | — | | — | . |

record.....record　　　　use......use　　　　loose ....lose
decrease...decrease　　　　　　　　　　　close........close
present....present
rebel.......rebel

E

Listen to these words. Underline the *longest* syllable.

extend	wider	require
inform	over	gather
arrive	campus	unit

F

Dictation. Listen to these sentences and write the words that are missing.

1. Oh, did you _____ something?

2. Pack the _____ into the _____.

3. I think this handle is _____.

4. What _____ to fix a _____?

5. They haven't _____ our _____ yet.

17

Self-analysis

Record these words several times and then check your accuracy in the length of the syllables.

1. be͞e be̍at u͞se (verb) u̍se (noun) lo̍ose lo͞ose

2. lo͞aded̍ allo͞w

3. pre͞sent̍ (noun) pre̍sent͞ (verb)

4. We want to reco̍rd͞ that music. We want a re͞cord̍ of that music.

Was there a clear contrast between the short and long syllables?

4 · Stress: clarity

English has two kinds of vowels: clear and unclear. The contrast between clear and unclear vowels is essential to the language.

Stressed syllables *always* have clear vowels. Unstressed syllables *usually* have unclear vowels.

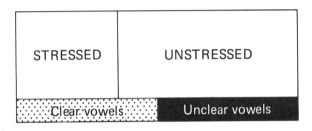

STRESSED	UNSTRESSED
Clear vowels	Unclear vowels

Listen to this word:

banana

Now listen again and decide which syllable has the full, clear vowel sound:

banana   banana

The word "banana" is written with three letter "a" vowels. But only one "a" is said with a full, clear sound. The other two letter "a" vowels are said with a reduced, unclear sound. This vowel sound is very short.

bánaná   Canádá   Alábamá

Note: The unclear vowels are the most commonly used vowel sounds in English.

Rule: All stressed vowels are clear.

Clear vowels	Unclear vowels
full (long) can be stressed	reduced (short) cannot be stressed

A

Listen to the following words. Which syllable has the reduced, unclear vowel? Draw a line through it. Example:

bánaná

printed   límit
landed   wátches
dráma   rented
mélted   fínish
bóttom   mésses

B

Listen and then practice contrasting clear and unclear vowels.

1. *Clear vowel   Clear vowel + unclear vowel*

   Tom ....atóm
   man..........womán
   men..........womén

2. *Clear vowel   Unclear vowel + clear vowel(s)*

   add...........áddition
   pot...........pótato
   atóm..........átomic
   office.........ófficial

C

Listen to the names of these states. Practice contrasting the clear and unclear vowels.

1 clear vowel   2 clear vowels

Névadá   New York
Michigán   Alábamá
Kansás   Okláhomá
Texás   Minnésotá

D

Listen and then practice clarity for the stressed vowels in the following words, being careful to make a contrast with the unclear vowels.

atóm   presént (noun)   Américá
átomic   présent (verb)   Britáin
recórd (noun)   ágo   Englánd
récord (verb)   sofá   Canádá
objéct (noun)   Árabiá   Chiná
óbject (verb)   Jápan   Brázil

E

Some clear vowels are not stressed. Examples:

INdex   mainTAIN   MAILbox   AIRport   PASSport

Listen and then practice saying the following words and sentences, being careful to make a contrast between clear and unclear vowels.

1. CONtrast   cónTRAST   CONtest   cónTEST
   CONtract   cónTRACT   EXtract   éxTRACT
2. They make vanilla EXtract by éxTRACTing the essence of vanilla.
   It was a big CONtest, and she plans to cónTEST the decision.

F	🔲

Listen to these words. Underline the full vowels.

campus   professor   photograph
college   seminar   photography
degree   registration   semester

Summary

Stressed syllables	1. have a higher pitch than	**unstressed syllables**
↓	2. are longer than	↓
only clear vowels		mostly unclear vowels

The practical effect of this rule is that you need to concentrate only on the stressed vowels.

G	🔲

Dictation. Listen to these sentences and write the words that are missing.

1. There's always an _____ at the end of the _____.
2. We _____ three states: _____, _____, and

   _____.

3. She's going to _____ two places: _____ and _____.
4. You've got to spend _____ of time in _____ for any

   profession.
5. _____ vowels are never _____.

Self-analysis

Record these words several times and then check your accuracy for the three signals of stress: pitch change, length, and clarity.

about   asleep   drama   woman   women   photograph   photography

5 · Review

Syllables

Listen and then say these words. On which words is the final "es" or "ed" pronounced as an added syllable?

added	proposes	wanted	wiped
caused	pointed	poses	recommended
shouted	developed	mixes	mixed
checked	announces	attached	advances
advanced	happens	wasted	opposes
happened	avoided	described	acted

Pitch patterns

Listen to these common American names. Draw a pitch line for each name. This can help you hear unfamiliar words better. Example:

Angelica

Tom   Jeanie   Anthony   Ellen

Jerome   Victoria   Elaine

Length of vowel

Listen and then practice contrasting vowel lengths.

longer   shorter   · —   — ·

why .....white	review	basis
so ....soap	around	rocket
may .....mate	preserve	cousin
cue ......cute	attend	answer
sea ......seat	arrive	tourist

Clarity of vowel 📼

Listen and then practice contrasting the clear and unclear vowels in the
names of these U.S. states.

1 clear vowel	*2 clear vowels*	*3 clear vowels*
Florída	Arízoná	New Mexíco
Névadá	Minnésotá	North Caróliná
Nébraská	Tennéssee	South Caróliná
Georgía	Utah	thé Unitéd States
Iówá	North Dákotá	

Self-analysis

Record the names of the states in the previous section. Did you stress the correct syllable? Was there a definite contrast between clear and unclear vowels?
Were the stressed vowels lengthened?

Summary: stressed syllable signals

1. *Pitch change*	record record
	economy economic
2. *Length*	atom atomic banana

3. *Clarity*
  a. Most unstressed vowels are unclear.
  b. ALL STRESSED VOWELS ARE
     CLEAR.
	regísTRAtión
	tó thé STAtión

6 · *Stress patterns*

 When you hear a new word, the first thing you should notice is its stress pattern. Listen to this very long word:

      microcontaminants

Did you hear

1. MIcrocónTAmínánts   or   2. miCROcóntaMInánts?

Every English word has a stress pattern. This pattern is part of the word's proper pronunciation. If you place a stress on the wrong syllable, it may be hard for other people to understand you. Knowing the stress pattern is part of knowing the word.

| A |

Listen and then repeat these words.

1st syllable	*2nd syllable*	*3rd syllable*
ENGlish	staTIStics	engiNEERing
CHEMistry	eLECtrical	elecTRIcity
INdustry	inDUStrial	uniVERsity
MANagement	reSPONsible	regisTRAtion
MAjor	geOgraphy	impliCAtion

| B |

Words often have a different stress pattern when they have a different grammatical function. Therefore, the pattern is a grammatical signal to the listener. Listen and then practice these words.

REgister ......regisTRAtion
adMINister...adminisTRAtion

eXAmine .....examiNAtion

SPEcialize.....specialiZAtion

biOlogy.......bioLOgical
geOlogy.......geoLOgical
biOgraphy....bioGRAPHical
techNOlogy ..technoLOgical
AGriculture...agriCULtural
elecTRIcity....eLECtrical

| C |

Listen to these technical words. Underline the most stressed syllable.

24

personality	pathogenic
mammalian	metabolic
analytical	calculus
pharmacology	

D

Listen to the following word pairs. Are the stress patterns in both words the same or different? Write "S" or "D." Example:

winter summer *S* open around *D*

1. under over —
2. question answer —
3. require offer —
4. Alaska Nebraska —
5. correction institute —
6. certificate delivery —
7. considerably manufacturer —
8. absolutely recovery · —
9. expensive requirement —
10. specify separate —

Note: The majority (75%) of two-syllable words are stressed on the first syllable. If you count only nouns and adjectives (no verbs), it is 90%.

This is also likely to be true for American names. Practice saying these names with the stress on the first syllable.

First names	*Last names*	
Susan	Burton	Reagan
Roger	Brady	Carter
Janet	Miller	Lincoln
Thomas	Simpson	Redford
Robert	Wagner	Newman

E

"Two-word verbs" are very common in American English. They can also be used as nouns. The stress is usually on the first part for a noun and on the second part for a verb. Practice saying the following words, making the difference in stress.

Noun	*Verb*
a SET up (an arrangement)	to set UP (to arrange)
an UPset (a disturbance)	to upSET (to disturb)
a TAKEoff (what happens when a plane leaves the ground)	to take OFF (to leave the ground, to take off clothes, to leave)
a PUT on (informal: a joke)	to put ON (to put on clothes)
a TURN on (informal: something that excites you)	to turn ON (to turn on lights, the TV, radio, etc.)
a TURN off (informal: something you do not like)	to turn OFF (to turn off the radio, etc.)
a LOOK out (a high place from which to see better, a sentry)	to look OUT (to be careful)

F

Here are more two-word verbs (and their noun versions) for you to practice saying.

Noun	Verb
stopover	stop over
trade-in	trade in
handout	hand out
makeup	make up
dropout	drop out

G

Dictation. Listen to the following sentences and write the missing words.

1. _____ got _____ when he talks to his boss.

2. _____ often gone up _____.

3. Do you think _____ going _____ with us?

4. _____ important _____ the motor when you're

   waiting _____.

Self-analysis

Record the following words, then check yourself for accuracy.

register.......registration
biology.......biological
history.......historical
agriculture...agricultural
economy.....economic
technology...technological

a turn on...to turn on
an upset....to upset
a record....to record

They're studying agricultural economics.

Did you stress the right syllables? Do not emphasize unstressed syllables.

7 · English rhythm

Each language has its own rules for rhythm. Clear English speech depends on the way varying lengths of syllables produce a characteristic rhythm. You will be much easier to understand if you use English rhythm.

Syllable rhythm rules

1. Clear vowels are full (long). Unclear vowels are reduced (short).

   above   along   around

2. Vowels in succession are usually of different lengths.

   a. mama   banana   Alaska   Nebraska

   b. a basket   the record

   c. absolute   Have some fruit.   impossible   It's possible.

3. When two or more full vowels are spoken in succession, length is added to each vowel. This makes the speech sound emphatic (strong).

   passport   mailbox   airport   maintain

   Listen and then practice saying these sentences.

   a. Get out!   e. Jean likes plain soap.
   b. Please bring food.   f. Fish don't eat grass.
   c. Hold up those lights.   g. Jane can't do that!
   d. Don't talk nonsense!   h. Jack won't tell George.

A

You will hear ten sentences. Do you hear a succession of full vowels, or is the sentence made of vowels of different lengths? Put a checkmark under the description for each sentence.

	All full vowels	*Vowels of different lengths*
1.	√	
2.		
3.		
4.		
5.		
6.		
7.		

All full vowels   *Vowels of different lengths*

8.
9.
10.

B	

Listen to the following limerick and then practice the rhythm.

> A STUdent was SENT to TaCOma*
> inTENding to EARN a diPLOma.
> He SAID, "With the RAIN,
> I don't WANT to reMAIN.
> I THINK I'd preFER OklaHOma."**

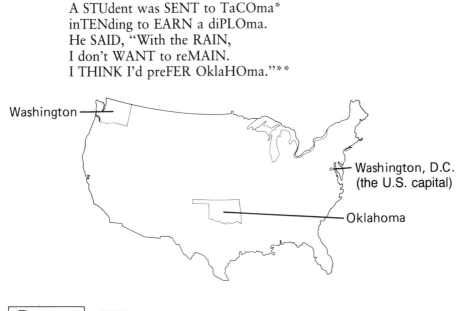

C	

In the following sentences, the last three words are dramatically slowed down because there are three full vowels in succession. Listen and then practice saying them.

1. Give me your permission to go right now.
2. We're all very proud of that fine old man.
3. The government intends to stop all strikes.

D	

Listen and then practice the rhythm of the following words.

3 syllables

redúctión   frústratión
súggestión   córrectión
íntentión

4 syllables

oppósitión   dedícatión
oblígatión   intéractión
regístratión

---

*Tacoma, Washington, is an exceptionally rainy city.
**Oklahoma is an exceptionally dry state.

8 · Review

Stress patterns 🔲

Listen and then practice saying these words.

1	2	3
relative	agreement	economic
photograph	photography	automatic
discipline	arrangement	indication
agency	participate	argumentative
anyhow	alternative	absolutely

English rhythm

A word said by itself is like a small sentence. It must have all the rhythm and emphasis of a sentence. 🔲 Listen and then practice saying the following "pairs."

Word stress   *Sentence emphasis*

1. atTRACtive . . . . It's ACtive.
2. absóLUTE . . . . Have sóme FRUIT.
3. réSPONsíble . . . . It's POSSíble.
4. electríficATión . . . . . She went tó thé STAtión.

Limerick 🔲

Listen and then practice the following nonsense verse. Tap the emphasized syllables to be sure of the rhythm.

I KNEW a MAN from ARkanSAS*
who ATE a ROCK that BROKE his JAW.
"WHAT do you THINK?"
he SAID, with a WINK,
"PerHAPS it's BAD to EAT them RAW."

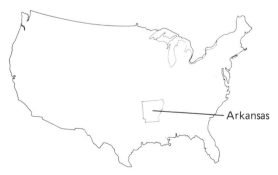
— Arkansas

*Pronounced "Arkansaw."
wink: to close one eye, meaning "this is a joke"
raw: uncooked
jaw: the lower part of the mouth

5 syllables		*6 syllables*	*8 syllables*
ádminístratión	claríficatión	identíficatión	intérnatiónálizatión
éxaminatión	justíficatión	reínterprétatión	
simplíficatión		reuníficatión	

E	[cassette]

Listen and then practice the rhythm of these sentences.

1. There's been á réductión.
2. She made á súggestión.
3. There's á lot óf oppósitión.
4. How high áre thé prícés?
5. Á passport shows identíficatión. (some people say "ídentíficatión")

Self-analysis

Record the limerick in B above. Are you lengthening the stressed syllables?
Be careful not to give emphasis to any of the other syllables.

THOUGHT UNITS

9 · Reductions

Unemphasized words become more and more reduced as speech becomes more rapid or more informal. Not only do vowels reduce in length, but some consonants also reduce. The sound "h" can even disappear completely. Examples:

Slow, formal	*Rapid, informal*
I have gone	I've gone
they have	they've
is he	is (h)e (rhymes with "busy")
give her	give (h)er (rhymes with "liver")
would he	would (h)e (sounds like "woody")

Reduction is a fundamental characteristic of English and helps explain why written English is so different from spoken English.

A

Listen to these sentences. Which version did you hear, (a) or (b)? Practice saying them.

1a. Did (h)e go?
 b. Did she go?
2a. Is (h)e here?
 b. Is she here?
3a. Give (h)im the book.
 b. Give (h)er the book.

4a. Send (h)im the pen.
 b. Send me the pen.
5a. Is (h)er work good?
 b. Is our work good?

B

Note: The letter "h" is not reduced when the pronoun is especially emphasized or comes at the beginning of a sentence. In these cases the pronoun must be very clear.

Listen and practice saying these sentences.

1a. Her ideas are brilliant.
 b. His plan is excellent.
2a. She works hard.
 b. He works hard.

3a. I don't want HER pen; I want HIS pen. (contrast)
 b. YOU'RE tall, but HE'S taller.
4a. They want HER. (special emphasis, or contrast)
 b. They want HIM.

C 🔲

Listen and then practice reducing pronouns.

1. When did (h)e go there?
2. Who did (h)e talk to?
3. Have you talked to (h)im yet?
4. Where's (h)er homework?
5. Why does (h)e always come late?

6. Did you ask (h)er?
7. Did you ask (h)er where she was?
8. Did you ask (h)im where he was?
9. He says that it's none of your business.
10. He says that it's none of (h)er business.

D

These are some of the different uses for the word "have."

main verb:	I have a watch.
auxiliary:	I have bought a watch.
have to (must):	I have to buy a watch.

Rule: In American English, only the auxiliary use of "have" is reduced.
The other forms use a full vowel and keep the "h" sound. Examples:

Main verb	*Auxiliary*	*Have to (must)*
She has three sisters.	I've bought a watch.	We have to go now.
	We've listened carefully.	
	They've asked for food.	

Draw a line thorugh the letter "h" for the auxiliary verb "have" in the following sentences. Do not reduce the other uses of "have." Practice saying the sentences.

1. Do you think he has gone?
2. Where have they been?
3. How long have you been here?
4. I have to do some work now.

5. Do you think she has gone yet?
6. University students have to work hard.
7. You have done enough.
8. He has six classes.

Note: Auxiliaries (is, will, have, etc.) are *not* contracted in formal written English, but they usually *are* contracted in the spoken language and in informal writing. Contractions are used to reduce the less important words. This helps to emphasize the more important words.

Formal	*Informal*	*Formal*	*Informal*
I am	I'm	I would	I'd
We are	we're	I will	I'll
you are	you're	I have	I've
he is	he's	they have	they've
that is	that's		

E

Dictation. Listen to these sentences and write them exactly as they are spoken. Underline the contractions.

1. _____ .
2. _____ .
3. _____ .
4. _____ .
5. _____ .

F

When an auxiliary verb comes at the end of a sentence, it cannot be contracted, because the word was placed there to give it emphasis. Draw a line through sounds that should be reduced and then practice saying these sentences.

1. No, I do not think she has.
2. Yes, I have.
3. I think you are.

4. Maybe they will.
5. He is sure that they will bring some.
6. He is sure that they will.

G

Dictation. Listen to these sentences. Write them as you listen.

1. _____ .
2. _____ .
3. _____ .
4. _____ .
5. _____ .
6. _____ .
7. _____ .
8. _____ .
9. _____ .
10. _____ .

Self-analysis

Record the sentences from the dictation. Check for the presence or absence of the "h" sound, and all contractions.

10 · Basic emphasis pattern

Native speakers of American English use a basic pattern of emphasis. If you use this pattern, it will be much easier for other people to understand you.

In most English sentences, content words are emphasized and structure words are reduced. Any change in this pattern may change the meaning.

BASIC EMPHASIS PATTERN				
CONTENT WORDS (emphasized)	*nouns,* (cat)	*main verbs,* (runs)	*adverbs,* (quickly)	*adjectives* (happy)
STRUCTURE WORDS (not emphasized)	*pronouns,* (he, she)	*prepositions,* (of, to, at)	*articles,* (a, the)	*"to be"* verbs (is, was)
	conjunctions, (and, but)	*auxiliary verbs* (can, have, do, will)		

 A word is emphasized by emphasizing the stressed syllable. Listen to these examples.

1. I WANT a baNANa.
2. The proFESsor is FAmous.
3. The WORKer is COMing.
4. She's WRITten a PAper.
5. It's DIFficult to underSTAND.
6. He's PLANning to GRAduate.

A

Listen to this limerick again. Underline the content words. Then read the limerick out loud. Notice how the rhythmic emphasis falls on the content words.

A student was sent to Tacoma
intending to earn a diploma.
He said, "With the rain,
I don't want to remain.
I think I'd prefer Oklahoma."

B

Underline the content words in the following sentences.

1. Do you like the picture on your passport?
2. Did you take a test for a driver's license in this country?

3. Students pay a lot of money for their books, don't you think?
4. Do you think it is harder to speak or to hear a foreign language?
5. Is there a speed limit for cars in your country?

Self-analysis

Read the following dialogue. Underline the content words. Then record yourself saying this dialogue aloud several times.

X: What's the matter?
Y: I lost my keys.
X: Where'd you put them?
Y: If I knew, I could find them!

11 · Review

Reduction

Dictation. Listen to the following sentences. Write them as you listen.

1. _____ .
2. _____ .
3. _____ .
4. _____ .
5. _____ .

Basic emphasis pattern

Listen to this nonsense verse and underline the content words. Practice the rhythm.

Too Small for a Whole Grammar

The size of the state of Connecticut*
affects our grammatical etiquette.
To be extra polite,
a Subject's all right,
but the space is too small for a Predicate.

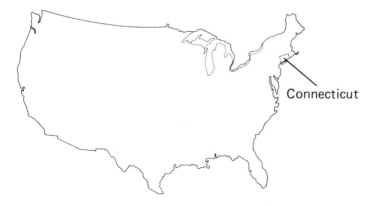

Connecticut

*The second "c" in Connecticut is silent.
etiquette: good manners

12 · Sentence focus (part 1)

FOCUS FOCUS FOCUS FOCUS FOCUS FOC

OCUS FOCUS FOCUS FOCUS **FOCUS** FO

S FOCUS FOCUS FOCUS FOCUS FOCUS

FOCUS FOCUS FOCUS FOCUS FOCUS F

There are different ways to express emphasis in a sentence. Each one changes the *focus* of the sentence.

Basic pattern

1. Basic Emphasis Rule:
   a. Content words emphasized
   b. Structure words not emphasized
   example: I LOST my HAT.
2. The most important word has the most emphasis. This word is the *sentence focus*.
   example: What KIND of hat?
3. When a conversation begins, the focus word is usually the final content word. Examples:
   Where should we EAT?
   Where are you GOing?
   I missed the BUS.

New focus

You can emphasize any word in a sentence, if you want to call attention to a *new idea* or make a special contrast with an idea that was talked about before.

A   🔲

Listen to these dialogues.

Dialogue 1

X: I lost my HAT. (basic emphasis pattern: final content word is the focus)
Y: What KIND of hat? (<u>hat</u> is now an old idea. <u>kind</u> is the new focus)
X: It was a RAIN hat.
Y: What COLOR rain hat?

X: It was WHITE. White with STRIPES.
Y: There was a white hat with stripes in the CAR.
X: WHICH car?
Y: The one I SOLD.

Dialogue 2

X: I want some SHOES.
Y: What KIND of shoes?
X: CAsual shoes.
Y: BLACK or BROWN?
X: NEIther. I'm TIRED of black and brown. I want RED shoes. SHIny red shoes.

B

Practice saying these dialogues, following the same focus pattern.

Dialogue 1

A: Where are you going?
B: Europe.
A: Where in Europe? To the north or to the south?
B: Neither. I've already been north and south. I'm going east.

Dialogue 2

X: What've you been doing?
Y: I've been studying.
X: Studying what? Math or English?
Y: Neither. I'm sick of math and English. I'm studying nutrition, because I'm always hungry.

C

Practice responding aloud to the following statements. Emphasize new focus words in order to show contrast with the idea in the first statement.

1. Moscow is a COUNtry.   No, that's WRONG. It's a CIty.
2. Paris is in ENGland.   No, that's WRONG. It's in FRANCE.
3. Dallas is in CaliFORnia.   No, that's WRONG. It's in TEXas.

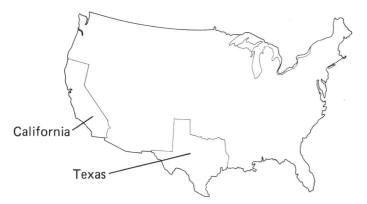

California

Texas

Before continuing with the following sentences, read them silently and decide which word needs to be emphasized in order to call attention to the contrasting ideas. Underline one word in each sentence, then practice saying the
statement and the response.

4. This is my book.   No, it's his book.
5. She wrote that article.   No, I wrote it.
6. Classes finish on the sixteenth.   No, I think they finish on the fifteenth.
7. The keys are on the desk.   No, they're in the desk.
8. He's speaking to Marie.   No, he's speaking about Marie.
9. They sell books in the library.   No, they sell books in the bookstore.
   They lend books in the library.
10. He can write well.   He can, but he doesn't. Too lazy. (underline two
    words in second sentence)

D

Practice responding to these different statements.

1a. It's a big DOG.   No, it's a BEAR.
 b. It's a BIG dog.   No, it's a LITtle one.
2a. I suppose you're flying from BraZIL?   No, I'm flying from PeRU.
 b. I suppose you're flying FROM Brazil?   No, I'm flying TO Brazil.
3a. But we asked for two COKES!   Well, I thought you wanted COFfee.
 b. But we asked for TWO Cokes!   Well, I thought you wanted ONE.

E

Practice saying the following dialogue. Substitute your own new information
(new focus) for the words in parentheses.

X: Are you from (CaliFORnia)?
Y: No, I'm from (JaPAN).
X: How long've you LIVED here?
Y: I've lived here (three MONTHS).
X: What're you STUDying?
Y: I'm studying (CHEMistry).
X: Oh, that's what (BECKy's) studying. (She) says it's EAsy.
Y: It may be easy for (HER), but it's NOT easy for ME.

F

Listen to this dialogue and underline the focus words. Then practice saying it.
(Different people might emphasize different words.)

X: Do you think American food's expensive?
Y: Not really.
X: Well, I think it's expensive.
Y: That's because you eat in restaurants.
X: Where do you eat?
Y: At home.
X: I didn't know you could cook.

Y: Well, actually I can't. I just eat bread and Coke.
X: That's awful!
Y: No, it isn't. I like bread and Coke.
X: You're crazy!

G

Underline the focus words and practice saying this dialogue.

A: Hi! What's new?
B: Nothing much. What's new with you?
A: I'm going to Washington.
B: Washington State or Washington, D.C.?
A: D.C. I want to see the capital.

H

Listen to these questions and underline the focus words. Then ask someone else the questions. The answers can be one or two words, and they should respond to the focus word in the question.

1. When did you arrive here?
2. Where did you get your English book?
3. Who told you how to get a visa?
4. What languages can you speak?
5. Which language is the most difficult to learn?
6. Do you think it is harder to speak or to hear a foreign language?

Self-analysis

Record the dialogue in ⛶F. Did you emphasize the focus words? Did you definitely *not* emphasize the old ideas (old focus words)? The contrast between emphasis and lack of emphasis must be clear.

Summary

How to call the listener's attention to what you think is important:

SENTENCE EMPHASIS	
Basic emphasis pattern	Content words are emphasized. Structure words are generally not emphasized. *example:* We WANT a baNAna.
Focus	The final content word in a sentence usually has the most emphasis. *example:* She wants some SHOES.
New focus	Any word that gives new information is the new focus in a conversation. *example:* What KIND of shoes? The CAsual kind.

13 • *The importance of focus*

Most sentences follow the basic emphasis pattern. If an English speaker changes the pattern, there is always a reason: The speaker wants the listener to notice the unusual emphasis.

A

Read the following story, which is based on the above principle.

*The Conversation**

Several years ago, in San Francisco, there was a rich man with a young wife. This man was suspicious of his wife and wanted to know what she did during the day. He hired a private detective to follow her. The detective found out that every Friday, just at the noon hour, she met a young man and they walked around and around Union Square, in the downtown business section. The rich husband ordered the detective to make a tape recording of their conversation. This was very difficult, because there were always a lot of people in the Square at noon and, besides, the young couple always kept walking. They never stood still or sat down. The detective decided that they were afraid of being noticed. Perhaps they were even afraid of being recorded. But he was very clever and had good recording equipment, so he was able to record their conversation from the top of a building nearby.

What were they saying? The tape was so noisy that the only thing the detective could understand was that they were planning a special meeting at 2 p.m. on the next Sunday, at the Jack Tar Hotel. This worried him, because he knew that the husband was already jealous. Clearly the young couple were lovers. All Saturday, the detective worked on the tape with his electronic equipment. All the time he worked, he was getting more and more worried. Was the young woman in danger? What would the husband do if he found out about their plans? The detective felt that he might be responsible for a tragedy. But he kept working on the tape. Finally, he was able to make one sentence clear. The young woman was saying,

"If he gets the chance, he'll KILL us!"

This was exactly what the detective had been afraid of. So he decided not to give the tape of the conversation to her husband. But Saturday night, the tape was stolen. Surely the husband must have it! The detective was in a panic. How could he save her life?

*This story is taken from an American movie, *The Conversation*.

41

On Sunday, the detective rushed to the Jack Tar Hotel, well before 2 p.m. But he was too late. There were police in front of the hotel, and an ambulance was waiting. The police were carrying a dead body out of the front doors. The detective was struck with horror and guilt. Then he was confused. The dead body was not the wife, but the husband! What had happened?

Then the detective saw the young wife standing near the ambulance. She had a very small smile on her face. This little smile made the detective think carefully. He realized that he had completely misunderstood the whole conversation. Because he had been so sure that the young woman was in danger, he had thought he heard her say,

"If he gets the chance, he'll KILL us!"

If he had listened to the tape with an open mind, he would have heard what she really said:

"If he gets the chance, HE'll kill US!"

They were the same words, but with a completely different meaning. This was not a conversation between frightened lovers. It was a plan to commit murder.

B

The clue to the murder plot is this: The basic emphasis pattern was not followed. Instead of emphasizing the main verb, the wife emphasized the pronouns. This unusual emphasis means that the pronouns were in contrast to pronouns that must have been discussed earlier in the conversation.

Basic emphasis pattern	He'll KILL us!
Special emphasis	HE'll kill US!

C

Fill in the blank:

Earlier in the conversation, the wife must have said something like: "We'll KILL _____."

14 · Sentence focus (part 2)

Procedure for these exercises

Read the paragraph silently. Then underline the focus words. Practice reading each paragraph aloud, emphasizing the focus words.

Remember, people can have different opinions about the focus of ideas. Decide what *you* think is important.

A

It is a lot of trouble to learn a new language. When we go to all that trouble, we certainly want to be understood. But understanding is based on more than speech. Sometimes misunderstanding comes not from the wrong words, but from the wrong style. In our own country, we learn the style for politeness. But this polite style may be misunderstood in another country. This can cause unexpected difficulties. Since you have spent so much effort learning this new language, it is sensible and practical to learn the politeness rules also. Even if you think some of the customs are foolish, learning them can help you to be clearly understood.

B

In your country, is it considered polite to listen quietly to other people, without any change of expression on the face? If this is the style you have learned, perhaps you should watch two Americans talking. Notice how the person who is listening will have frequent changes of expression. The listener may also make little remarks while the other person is talking. These little remarks may be one word, like "Really?" or they may just be a little sound, like "uh-huh" or "mmm." This is the way American listeners show that they are listening in a friendly way. That is why Americans get uneasy when the listener is silent and shows no change of expression. In the American style of speaking, an unmoving face often means that the listener is unfriendly, or perhaps even angry.

C

Sometimes people from two cultures are uncomfortable with each other for very small reasons. Here is an example: Americans think that perspiration (sweat) odor is not polite. In fact, they worry so much about this subject that they spend a great deal of money on deodorants and dry cleaning and washing their clothes. If a foreign student does not follow the same rule, Americans may be disturbed and think the foreigner is not nice. The problem can be especially troublesome because Americans are so embarrassed about this subject that they do not even like to talk about it, so they are not likely to tell that person why they are uneasy.

15 • Questions

Every language has ways to show the difference between a question and a statement. English has two ways:

1. Question word (Why, Who, etc.)
2. Rising pitch at the end

   Questions with a question word generally end in a falling pitch. Questions that can be answered with yes or no generally end with a rise.

| A |  |

Listen to the pitch patterns of the following questions.

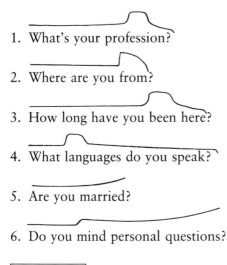

1. What's your profession?

2. Where are you from?

3. How long have you been here?

4. What languages do you speak?

5. Are you married?

6. Do you mind personal questions?

| B |

Read the following questions aloud. Draw pitch patterns and then practice saying the questions.

1. Where is your family?

2. Do you have children?

3. How many do you have?

4. How old are they?

5. Do they go to school?

6. What kind of school?

7. Are you pleased with the school?

16 · Thought groups

 English speakers use pauses and pitch fall to mark the end of thought groups.

A

When you read numbers aloud over the telephone (addresses, telephone numbers, passport numbers, etc.), it is important to group the terms correctly.
Listen to the following series of numbers. Then practice pauses to mark the end of each group.

1a. 5282   0149
 b. 52 82 01   49
2a. 95   616
 b. 95   61   6
3a. 916   756   5183
 b. 916   7565   183

Take turns testing the class. Did you read (a) or (b)?

B

Practice saying the following sentences, using pauses to mark the end of a group.

1. Raisins are good,   but dates are better.
2. He buys the groceries   and then cooks the dinner.
3. They bought me some candy,   and then they ate it themselves.
4. White bread is okay,   but I prefer whole wheat.
5. Food is a good topic,   especially around noon.

C

Listen to the following equations. Then practice saying them, using pauses and fall in pitch to show the end of each group.

1. $(A + B) \times C = Y$ (A plus B times C equals Y)

2. $A + (B \times C) = D$ (A plus B times C equals D)
3. $A - (B \times C) = Y$

4. $(A - B) \times C = Y$
5. $(X \div Y) - A = B$

D

Practice saying these problems. The correct answer depends on correct grouping.

1. $(2 + 3) \times 5 =$
2. $2 + (3 \times 5) =$
3. $3 \times (3 + 5) =$
4. $(3 \times 3) + 5 =$
5. $(3 - 2) \times 6 =$
6. $(4 - 2) \times 5 =$
7. $4 - (2 \times 5) =$
8. $(6 \div 2) \times 5 =$
9. $(16 \div 4) \times 2 =$
10. invent your own

E

Pitch patterns connect parts of a sentence. The connector words are usually low. The pitch pattern shows which parts of the sentence have a similar function. Listen and then practice saying these sentences.

1. They like both movies and concerts.

2. Exams are based on both the book and your notes.

3. She's going to study either math or physics.

4. We have to pay for tuition and also for books.

5. Effective study requires not only effort but skill.

F

Listen and then practice the different emphases in the following pairs of sentences. You must exaggerate the thought-group endings in order to distinguish these sentences, which are easily confused in speech.

1a. She likes pie and apples.

b. She likes pineapples.

2a. Do you want Super Salad?

b. Do you want soup or salad?

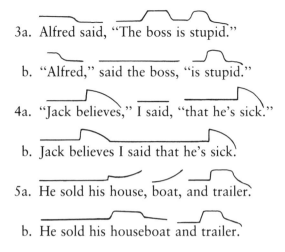

3a. Alfred said, "The boss is stupid."

 b. "Alfred," said the boss, "is stupid."

4a. "Jack believes," I said, "that he's sick."

 b. Jack believes I said that he's sick.

5a. He sold his house, boat, and trailer.

 b. He sold his houseboat and trailer.

What should you do if you cannot think of a word when you are in the middle of a thought group? Do not stop! Use the English "hesitation sound." This will fill the silence so that you do not have a pause, which would falsely signal the end of a group. Pauses in the wrong place confuse the listener.

   Practice filling the silence with "uh" or "mmm":

1. She wants...medicine right now.
2. I need the...tool that you bought.
3. The color is too...bright for me.
4. We can't...delay any more.
5. He broke the...switch on the TV.

   You can also fill pauses with words like "that thing," "that stuff," "the thing you use for fixing things." YOU DO NOT NEED TO STOP JUST BECAUSE YOU CANNOT THINK OF THE EXACT WORD.

Self-analysis

Record the sentence pairs in F above. Did you carefully distinguish between them?

17 • Review

Basic emphasis pattern 📼

Listen to the following sentences and underline the content words.

1. The rich man has a young wife.
2. The wife is meeting with the husband's assistant.
3. A detective has a tape of their conversation.
4. He is worried.
5. Is the husband planning to murder them?

Focus

The most important word is usually the final content word. 📼 Listen to these sentences and draw pitch lines for them. Practice saying them.

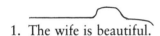

1. The wife is beautiful.

2. The assistant is young.

3. Is the husband jealous?   (be careful: this is a yes/no question)

4. They're planning to murder him.

5. The detective didn't really listen to it.

New focus 📼

Listen to the following conversation and underline the focus words. Notice the changes in focus.

POLICEMAN:	What are you doing here?
PRIVATE DETECTIVE:	I thought there was going to be a murder.
POLICEMAN:	Well, there has been. Did you know this man?
PRIVATE DETECTIVE:	I...mmm...I thought I did.
POLICEMAN:	Tell me what you know.
PRIVATE DETECTIVE:	I thought I knew a lot. But now I'm...confused.
POLICEMAN:	Mister, you're not making any sense. You'd better come with me.

Questions 🖭

Listen to these questions and draw pitch lines for them.

1. What's your name?

2. Where do you live?

3. Did you know the victim?

4. Why didn't you tell us?

5. Did you do it?

Thought groups 🖭

Listen and then practice saying these sentences with pauses to mark the thought groups.

1. Detective movies are popular, but so are comedies.
2. People can forget their troubles and have a good time.
3. Acting is an old profession because people love entertainment.
4. Some actors are in the newspapers all the time and make a lot of money, but rock stars probably make more.

CLARITY OF SOUNDS

18 • Voicing

In unstressed syllables, consonants are often reduced in clarity, just as vowels are reduced. However, in the stressed syllables of emphasized words, it is important to make the consonant sound clear.

One of the most basic distinctions between English sounds is *voicing*. To understand the meaning of this term, press your hands against your ears and make this sound:

>   sssssssssssssssssssssss (unvoiced)

Now, continuing to press your hands against your ears, make this sound:

>   zzzzzzzzzzzzzzzzzzzzz (voiced)

Another way to test the difference is to put your hand on your throat. You should feel a vibration for "zzzz" but not for "ssss." Try them both again until you can feel the difference. The vibration is called *voicing*. All English vowels are voiced.

A

Each pair of words below is made in exactly the same way except for voicing. Listen and then practice differentiating these words. Make a clear contrast.

Voiced *Unvoiced*

zoo ....Sue
lazy ....lacy
raising....racing
van........fan
leaving....leafing
either .....ether
game......came
bay........pay
do.........to

Listen to your teacher or a student read random words from the lists above. Identify which type of sound you hear, voiced or unvoiced.

B

Listen to the following statements. Then practice saying the statement and the correct response.

1. He <u>raised</u> a horse.   Where did he keep it?   (z)
    He <u>raced</u> a horse.   Did it win?   (s)
2. We need a good <u>president</u>.*   Help elect one.   (z)
    We need a good <u>precedent</u>.*   Let's set one.   (s)
3. She <u>prizes</u>** old books.   Doesn't she like new ones?   (z)
    She <u>prices</u>** old books.   Is that her job?   (s)

C

Practice contrasting the following English sounds, voiced and unvoiced.

Voiced   Unvoiced

buy..........pie
they..........think
van..........ban
dime.........time
zoo..........Sue
measure .....mesh
Jane.........chain
goat.........coat

Self-analysis

Say the following examples. Write "v" over the voiced consonants and "uv"
over the unvoiced consonants. Then record the words several times.

1. Sue, zoo   lacy, lazy   raising, racing

2. vine, fine   fat, vat   leaving, leafing

3. thank, then   thin, then   either, ether

4. We think that Sue is leaving sooner than we thought.

Did you make a clear difference between the voiced and unvoiced sounds?

---

*A precedent is something said or done that may serve as an example of what should
be done in the future. People *set* precedents. People *elect* presidents.

**"To prize" something is to like it very much. "To price" something is to decide on a
price for it.

19 · *Voicing and syllable length*

Difference in final voicing can cause a difference in the length of the syllable. The vowel before a voiced final consonant is likely to be longer. This helps the listener identify the final consonant.

Say the following pairs of words and practice the contrast.

Vowel shorter, *final consonant unvoiced*	*Vowel longer,* *final consonant voiced*
half	have
safe	save
leaf	leave
batch	badge
rich	ridge
excuse (noun)	excuse (verb)
use (noun)	use (verb)
proof (noun)	prove (verb)
rice	rise
peace	peas
lice	lies
pace	pays
bus	buzz
safe	save
Miss	Ms. (pronounced "Mizz")
close (adjective)	close (verb)
loose (adjective)	lose (verb)

B

Listen to single words read at random from the above lists. Identify the sounds as voiced or unvoiced.

C 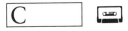

Listen to the following statements. Then practice saying the statement and the correct response.

1a. He wants peas.   Not carrots? (z)
 b. He wants peace.   Not war? (s)

2a. There's something in my eyes!   Call a doctor. (z)
  b. There's something in my ice!   Call a waiter. (s)

D

Americans generally do not pronounce the final sounds p/b, t/d, and k/g fully. You can identify the consonant by the length of the preceding vowel. For example, in the contrast "buck/bug," the vowel in "bug" is longer than the vowel in "buck." Listen and then practice the contrast in the following words.

voiced	d	g	b
unvoiced	t	k	p

bet ....bed   back...bag   cap....cab
sat ....sad   rack ...rag   mop...mob
debt...dead   rope...robe
feet ...feed

Self-analysis

Record the sentence pairs below. Check yourself for accuracy in distinguishing the voicing and length of syllables.

1a. She saw the place. (s)
  b. She saw the plays. (z)
2a. He wants peace. (s)
  b. He wants peas. (z)
3a. Did you say the noun "use"? (s)
  b. Did you say the verb "use"? (z)
4a. Does she call herself Miss Brown? (s)
  b. Does she call herself Ms. Brown? (z)

20 • Stops and continuants

Besides voicing, another fundamental distinction between English sounds is whether they are stop sounds or continuant sounds.

In some sounds, the air is stopped inside the mouth (stop sound). In other sounds, the air flows out without being stopped (continuant).*

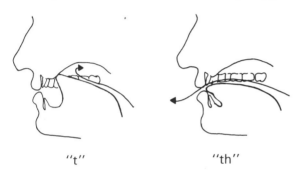

"t"   "th"

In stressed syllables, the exact identity of the sound is important, so you must learn to make the distinction between stops and continuants. This will also help you to hear spoken English more clearly.

To feel the difference between a stop and a continuant, make an "s" sound as long as you can. That is a *continuant* sound. Now make a "p" sound (not adding a vowel). Can you continue the "p"? No, because "p" is a *stop* sound.

Is the sound "th" a stop or a continuant? (see picture above)

The sounds of English

	Stops	Continuants
Voiced	boy, day, go, judge	me, then, low, row, vote, not, zoo, pleasure, and all vowels
Unvoiced	pan, too, cake chew	think, fine, say, shoe

*For a complete diagram of the mouth, see Unit 35, page 82.

56

The continuant sound in the picture below is an English "r." It does not stop the air flow. The stop sound is an English "d" or "t" (depending on the presence or absence of voicing).

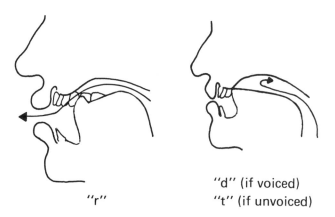

"r"

"d" (if voiced)
"t" (if unvoiced)

Say a word in your language with an "r" sound. Does the tongue touch the roof of the mouth? Even if you touch quickly, that stopping of the air flow will make an American listener think you said "d." To make an American "r" clearly, *the tip of the tongue must not touch.*

Say the following sounds. Practice *not* touching the tip of the tongue to the roof of your mouth.

ara   ara   aray   aray   aree   aree   aro   aro   aru   aru

Practice these contrasts.

Stops   Continuants

a deal...a real
I did ....I rid
a day....a ray
dead ....red
Dan .....ran
dot......rot
dough...row
doom ...room
dust .....rust

Practice contrasting the consonants p/f, ch/sh, t/th, t/s, b/v in the following pairs of words.

pat.....fat
chair...share
tank ...thank
tank ...sank
soup...Sue
boat ...bow
wrote..row
bake...bay
ban ....van

D

Listen to these questions. Then practice saying the questions and their answers.

1a. Do you like soup?   Only tomato.
 b. Do you like Sue?   Yes, she's nice.
2a. What are you watching?   A movie.
 b. What are you washing?   The dishes.
3a. What does "fine" mean?   Something like "good."
 b. What does "pine" mean?   A type of tree.
4a. What does "thought" mean?   The past tense of "think."
 b. What does "taught" mean?   The past tense of "teach."
5a. What's the date?   June first.
 b. What's the rate?   Twenty percent.
6a. What's a ram?   A male sheep.
 b. What's a dam?   A wall to hold water.
7a. Is it dead?   No, it's alive.
 b. Is it red?   No, it's orange.
8a. What does "ship" mean?   It's a boat.
 b. What does "chip" mean?   A small piece.
9a. Where's the vote?   On the paper.
 b. Where's the boat?   On the water.
10a. What's a van?   A kind of truck.
 b. What's a ban?   A prohibition.

E

Listen to these words. Which of the following columns of words ends with a continuant sound? Practice saying both groups.

1	*2*
have	cab
teethe	made
eyes	bag
half	cap
teeth	mate
ice	back

F

Listen and then practice contrasting stop and continuant endings.

wife.....wipe
both.....boat
bath.....bat
loathe...load
rove.....robe

Self-analysis

Record four of the sentence pairs in D. Check the distinction between stops and continuants.

21 • Puff of air (aspiration)

The unvoiced stops ("p," "t," and "k") have an extra signal to make the distinction between voiced and unvoiced sounds very clear. This signal is an extra puff of air. The puff of air is a help for clarity.

If you hold a piece of paper in front of your mouth, you can test yourself. The paper should move when you say a voiceless stop with a puff of air. The paper will not move without the puff of air. You can also test yourself by holding your hand in front of your mouth. You should feel the difference between the presence or absence of the puff of air.

A

Practice adding a puff of air.

o.....ho	eye...hi
ow...how	oo....who
ate...hate	ee....he

B

Rule: The unvoiced stops have an extra puff of air
– at the beginning of a word
– before a clear vowel.

This rule helps the listener know when a word in English begins or when a stressed syllable begins. The puff of air helps the listener notice the difference between voiced and unvoiced sounds. [cassette] Listen and then practice this difference by saying the following words.

1   2 (puff)

buy.....pie
bet......pet
down...town
done....ton
game...came
good....could

C

Listen to these questions. Then practice saying the questions and their correct responses.

1a. What's a bill?   Paper money.
 b. What's a pill?   Medicine.
2a. Where's the path?   Over the hills.
 b. Where's the bath?   In the bathroom.
3a. Is it gold?   No, it's silver.
 b. Is it cold?   No, it's hot.
4a. Do you have the time?   Yes, two o'clock.
 b. Do you have the dime?   No, did you lose it?
5a. What's a girl?   A young woman.
 b. What's a curl?   A twist of hair.

D

When the consonant sounds "p," "t," or "k" are said before a stressed vowel, aspiration is used to make the consonant very clear. Practice these contrasts

atóm....átomíc
recórd...récord
uppér....répair

When the stop consonant "t" is said between two vowels and the second vowel is reduced, the "t" sounds like a quick English "d." Listen to these examples.

little ("liddle")   atom ("adom")
city ("ciddy")   beautiful ("beaudiful")
bitter ("bidder")   Oh what a day! ("Oh, whadaday!")

Note: It is not necessary for you to use this "d" sound, but it is essential that you be able to recognize it, since it is common in informal speech (even that of educated Americans).

Self-analysis

Record the words below and check for the distinction between voiced and unvoiced stops.

1. bowl, pole   beat, Pete   ghost, coast   die, tie
2. I've got tó go.   I've caught a cold.
3. Tom, atóm, átomíc
4. recórd, récord

Did you use puffs of air for "p," "t," and "k"?

22 · Linking words

Most university students learn a foreign language mainly through the printed page. This produces a tendency to separate words during speech just as they are separated in print, an unfortunate tendency for people learning English. One of the essential characteristics of English is that the words in a thought group are linked together. If you practice linking words, your speech will become much clearer.

LINKS, LINKED TOGETHER IN A CHAIN

Listen and then practice saying the following linked groups, slowly at first, so that you can be sure that you are continuing a voiced vibration between the words. *Say the group as if it were one word.*

Vowel-to-vowel

my apple	she answers	we ought
high up	how old	you ought
no other	though I	may I
the end	too often	she is

B

When a word ends in a consonant, that final sound is often moved to the beginning of the next word, in order to maintain the smooth flow of linked words. Listen to these examples:

Is he busy?	sounds like	Izzybizzy?
take her out		take a route
send her		sender

Listen to these words. Then practice saying them.

Continuant-to-vowel

where I   will I

when I   can you

pull over   share it

push over   turn on

give up   plan everything

Stop-to-vowel

keep it	skip it	cube of	rob us	flag up
(kee pit)	(ski pit)	(cu bof)	(ro bus)	(fla gup)

break it	thank you	lend us	said it	stick out
(brea kit)	(than kyou)	(len dus)	(sai dit)	(sti ckout)

Stop-to-stop. Do not release the first consonant. Release the second. This stop takes more time.

Please stop pushing.   He opened the big gate.

Cook it in a deep pot.   He plans to rob both.

She has a black cat.   That's a bad dog.

Put ten in the box.   Where's the red door?

C

Listen to these groups. Then practice saying them, concentrating on linking.

1. She answers everything.   4. Send us out.

2. Wash all apples.   5. In a way, it's about taxes.

3. on all our exams   6. An athlete must keep practicing.

D

Practice linking words in the following sentences.

I plan to make an apple cake. I need four apples, an egg, a cup of sugar, three cups of flour, and a cube of butter. I hope Pat likes it!

E

In all countries, people play with language to make jokes. Try these "word plays" using linking:

Word play 1

I scream,
you scream,
we all scream
for ice cream.

Word play 2

Ask a friend to say this Liamese prayer (from the imaginary country of Liam)
very slowly and seriously. Then ask your friend to say it faster and faster.
When the words are fast and linked together, they make a joke. (The answer
is at the bottom of this page.)*

> OWA
> TAFU
> LIAM (pronounced "lie am")

Self-analysis

Record the sentences in D, and check yourself for linking and shifting consonants to the next word.

23 • Review

English rhythm 🔲

Listen to this limerick and then practice the rhythm. Notice that "quite hard" and "takes lots" are lengthened because they have full vowels in succession. This makes these words more emphatic.

> The teachers are quick to suggest
> that we study quite hard for a test.
> It takes lots of thought
> to learn what we're taught.
> But I think I prefer just to rest.

Clarity: voicing and length of syllable 🔲

Listen and then practice the following words. Lengthen the vowel before the final voiced sound.

have...........half	bed...bet
save...........safe	rag...rack
use (verb).....use (noun)	bug...buck
prove (verb)...proof (noun)	cab...cap
rode...........wrote	
close (verb)....close (adjective)	

Clarity: contrast between stops and continuants 🔲

Listen to these sentences and then practice saying them.

1a. What color is rust?   Usually orange.
 b. What color is dust?   Usually gray.
2. Tania thinks they teach that theory too much.

Clarity: puff of air 🔲

Listen to these word pairs and then practice saying them.

pan...ban	tie......die	came...game
pole...bowl	toe.....dough	could...good
pace...base	tense...dense	cash....gash

Reduction and linking

Dictation. Listen to the following sentences. Write them as you listen.

1. _____

2. _____

3. _____

4. _____

5. _____

LISTENING

24 • Listening accuracy

Procedure

1. Listen to the dictation once through as you read the script, so you can follow the meaning.
2. Listen to the dictation read slowly. Write what you hear.
3. After the dictation, check your accuracy with the script. Do you have all the content words right?
4. Check your control of the connection between pronunciation and spelling. If you had trouble with this, you should practice listening while you read.
5. Check for missing reduced words: articles (a, the), auxiliary verbs (was, should), and prepositions (of, for). If they are missing here, they are probably missing from your English, both in writing and in speech. This will affect the rhythm of your spoken English and will make your writing less effective.

Dictation

A study of one child showed that at as early as four months, he was using a basic sound of "m" as a sort of carrier for intonations when pointing at objects, varying the intonation according to whether the object was desired or merely wondered about. Can you think of any reason why intonation should be the first of the subsystems of language to develop?*

*From Bolinger, D. L., *Aspects of Language,* 2nd ed. (New York: Harcourt Brace Jovanovich, 1975), p. 10.

25 • Hearing numbers

Your new American friend is going to call on the telephone to give you the recipe for making one of America's most popular foods, *chocolate chip cookies*. Numbers can be hard to hear in a foreign language, so listen carefully. If you make a mistake with the numbers, the cookies might not taste good!

The measurements are given in American units, followed by metric units (cups, teaspoons, ounces, and Fahrenheit; milliliters, grams, and Celsius). (Transcript on page 92.)

Ingredients

—— cup or —— grams white sugar

—— cup or —— grams brown sugar

—— cup or —— grams butter

1 egg

—— teaspoon or —— ml vanilla

—— cups or —— grams flour

—— teaspoon or —— grams salt

—— teaspoon or —— grams baking soda

—— cup or —— grams nuts

—— ounces or —— grams chocolate chips

Method

Heat the oven to ——° Fahrenheit or ——° Celsius

Mix sugars, butter, egg, and vanilla thoroughly. Stir in remaining ingredients.

Drop dough by rounded teaspoonfuls about ——

inches or —— centimeters

apart on ungreased cookie sheet.

Bake —— to —— minutes

until light brown.

Cool slightly before removing from cookie sheet. This recipe makes about —— dozen cookies, which is —— individual cookies.

Dictate your telephone number and address to other students at the blackboard. Spell the name of your street. Did most of the students understand you correctly?

C

Listen to this short article and fill in the numbers.

Cookie business

Cookies are a big business in the U.S. One shop in Boston sells _____ warm cookies every day, mostly chocolate chip. On the West Coast, a ____ year-old American, Wally Amos, has made his fortune from chocolate chip cookies.

When Amos was ____ years old, he went to live with his Aunt Delia, who made cookies for him, from a recipe created in _____. Amos joined the Air Force in _____, and his aunt sent him cookies so he wouldn't be home-sick. For Amos, as for most Americans, cookies represent love and home.

After the Air Force, Amos worked for other people for ____ years. In _____, he decided he could make more money if he had his own busi-ness. He talked some friends into investing _____ in a cookie busi-ness. He worked _____ hours a day, baking cookies and thinking of clever ways to promote them. For instance, he traded _____ worth of cookies for advertising time on a local radio station. In _____, he began selling cookies in ____ department stores on the East Coast. That year the cookie corporation took in _____. By _____ the company made _____. Amos now has _____ employees, and they pro-duce more than _____ pounds of cookies a day.

26 • Getting essential information

When you ask for information, sometimes you get more than you need. It is important to listen for essential points, even if it means ignoring less important points.

Imagine that you are planning to visit Atlanta, Georgia. You will have to change from one airline to another in Chicago. The problem is that you will not have much time for the change. If you miss your Atlanta flight, you will have to spend the night in the Chicago airport. A friend has offered to tell you how to make the change quickly. A lot of this friend's advice may be useful, but only a few points are really essential.

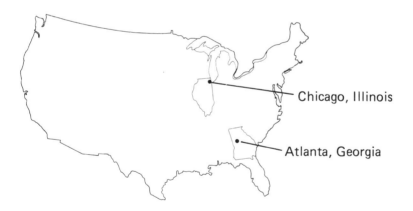

Vocabulary

arrivals: planes coming in
baggage claim: area where suitcases will arrive
departures: planes leaving
flight number: number of the plane
gate: place where the plane arrives or departs
security check: x-ray machine or baggage search
terminal: area for ticket counters and shops

📼   Listen to your friend's directions. Write in the missing information as you hear it.

Do you have a pencil and something to write on? O.K. Well, the first thing is that your plane will arrive at _____. When you come out of the gate, _____. Look for the signs that say _____ _____. If you follow those signs, you'll get to _____. Then you have to look for signs saying _____. Follow them until you get to the right terminal for Delta. Don't stop to buy a newspaper or anything because you won't have time. When you get to the _____ _____ , go through the security check. After the security check, keep going toward the Delta gates. You'll see TV screens for information up on the walls. Look for one that says Delta. The TV screens show all the arrivals and departures, but you just _____ for your Atlanta flight. Remember that your _____, and it's supposed to leave for _____. If you look _____ _____, you'll see the gate number. Then you better get there fast.

B

Answer the following questions:

1. What is the number of your arrival gate? _____
2. Which direction should you turn when you come out of the gate?

    _____
3. What sign should you look for first? _____
4. What terminal should you go to? _____
5. What sign should you look for in the terminal? _____
6. Where should you go through a security check? _____

    _____
7. What part of the screen should you look at? _____
8. What's your flight number? _____
9. When is it supposed to leave? _____
10. Where is the gate number? _____

C

Now look at the TV screens and the map of the Chicago airport. Draw a line from your arrival gate to your departure gate.

DELTA

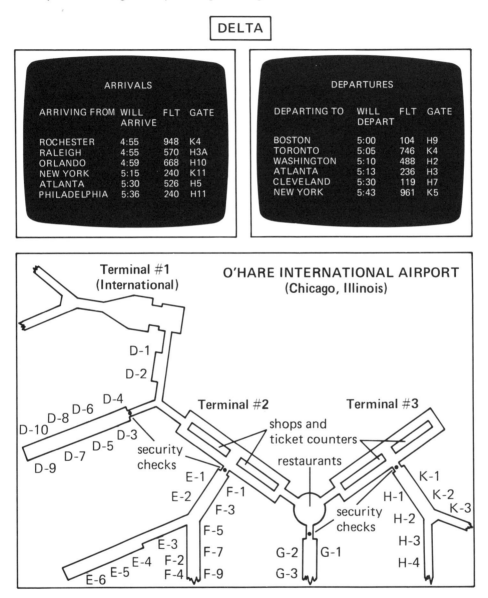

ARRIVALS			
ARRIVING FROM	WILL ARRIVE	FLT	GATE
ROCHESTER	4:55	948	K4
RALEIGH	4:55	570	H3A
ORLANDO	4:59	668	H10
NEW YORK	5:15	240	K11
ATLANTA	5:30	526	H5
PHILADELPHIA	5:36	240	H11

DEPARTURES			
DEPARTING TO	WILL DEPART	FLT	GATE
BOSTON	5:00	104	H9
TORONTO	5:05	746	K4
WASHINGTON	5:10	488	H2
ATLANTA	5:13	236	H3
CLEVELAND	5:30	119	H7
NEW YORK	5:43	961	K5

Terminal #1
(International)

O'HARE INTERNATIONAL AIRPORT
(Chicago, Illinois)

D-1
D-2
D-4
D-8 D-6
D-10
D-3
D-5
D-7
D-9
security checks

Terminal #2
shops and ticket counters
restaurants

Terminal #3

E-1
E-2
F-1
F-3
F-5
E-3
E-4 F-7
E-6 E-5 F-2
F-4 F-9
G-2 G-1
G-3
security checks
H-1
H-2
H-3
H-4
K-1
K-2
K-3

27 · *Listening comprehension (taking notes)*

Procedure

Listen to the following paragraphs once through, as you read the script. With your book closed, listen again and then write what you can remember of the paragraphs. Compare what you wrote with the script. Did you get all the main ideas?

One of the greatest difficulties for foreign students in American universities is the lecture system. The professor lectures and the students take notes. These notes are later used to study for examinations. If the notes aren't good, it will be hard for the student to prepare for a subsequent exam. It is not easy to take good notes from a lecture in a foreign language. If you try to write every word the professor says, then you are writing at the same time the professor is lecturing. This kind of note taking means that you will fall far behind the lecturer, and the notes will be confused. They may be useless for later study.

What can you do to take better notes? The first skill to learn is how to write only the most important words, not whole sentences. Significant words are the ones that present new information. The most important words are often the focus of intonation. They are usually emphasized by a pitch change, and this should be your signal of importance. Content words, like nouns and verbs, are usually the focus of information, so your notes should be almost entirely content words. Remember that you need information, not sentences.

28 • Listening comprehension: Age and Language Learning

Foreign language students often get upset when they hear a word they do not know. This reaction is damaging to comprehension, because it temporarily turns off the mind, so that the listener cannot hear the next words.

Your listening comprehension will be greatly improved when you learn to accept "blank spots" calmly, knowing that the idea may come clearly anyway. The words you miss may not be really important. If they are important, you may be able to guess their meaning from the words that follow.

A

Listen to this short talk, which is approximately the same length as the average TOEFL listening comprehension lecture. Do not read any material while you are listening, because it may interfere with your concentration. Afterward, take the brief examination in B and then check your comprehension by reading the talk (page 92).

Age and Language Learning

B

The most common type of university examination uses *multiple choice* questions. This type of exam is easily scored on a machine, and that is why it is used for large examination groups. On the following exam, use a pencil and be sure that you fill in the circle for your answer completely, so that a machine can "read" the answer. Also be sure that you completely erase any wrong answer. If any part of your erased mark can be seen, the machine may score the answer wrong.

Age and Language Learning

Choose one answer for each of the following questions.

1. The main idea in this short talk was that
   a. teenagers are more difficult to teach than adults.
   b. Danish teenagers can learn Swedish faster than younger children can.
   c. adults are more logical than children are.
   d. the ability to learn languages increases with age.

1. ⓐ ⓑ ⓒ ⓓ

2. This talk claimed that
   a. the ability to learn decreases with age.
   b. children are better language learners than adults.
   c. adults are able to learn more efficiently than children.
   d. teenagers learn less, in the same amount of time, than
      younger children.

2. ⓐ ⓑ ⓒ ⓓ

3. Which of the following possible explanations for older
   students' superior achievement was *not* mentioned?
   a. Adults know more about the world.
   b. Adults can use logical thinking.
   c. Adults have more self-discipline.
   d. Adults can read better.

3. ⓐ ⓑ ⓒ ⓓ

29 • Listening comprehension: Guides to Universities

In this exercise you will hear, but not see, a talk that is similar to, but longer than, talks given on the TOEFL examination. Listen to this talk. Do not read any material while you are listening, because it may interfere with your concentration. Afterward, check your comprehension by reading the talk (page 93).

Guides to Universities

You will hear, but not see, five questions. Stop the tape after each question. Choose the correct answer for each question and fill in the circle for the correct answer.

1a. different kinds of American universities
 b. sources of information about U.S. universities
 c. the difference between colleges and universities
 d. how to get accepted at a university   1. ⓐ ⓑ ⓒ ⓓ
2a. statistics about the American economy
 b. definitions of current slang expressions
 c. addresses of the schools
 d. current information   2. ⓐ ⓑ ⓒ ⓓ
3a. Catalogues give the names of the faculty members.
 b. There are too many details in the guidebook.
 c. Information in catalogues is current.
 d. Addresses are given for the dormitories.   3. ⓐ ⓑ ⓒ ⓓ
4a. textbooks
 b. students and faculty
 c. processing of applications for entrance
 d. payment for classes   4. ⓐ ⓑ ⓒ ⓓ
5a. the buildings where classes are held
 b. cafeterias
 c. the buildings where the students live
 d. transportation facilities   5. ⓐ ⓑ ⓒ ⓓ

30 • Lecture: Pronunciation Achievement Factors

A

Take notes while listening to this lecture. Then take the essay examination.

Pronunciation Achievement Factors

B

The *essay question* is a common type of test in American universities. The student is usually required to bring a Blue Book (a special examination booklet for writing the essay answers) into the examination room. All examinations have a time limit, so it is essential that you learn to write efficiently. Do not spend too much time on small details, because then you will not have enough time to write about the major points. Before you take this test, reread your notes from the lecture.

Pronunciation Achievement Factors

Choose *two* of the following questions and answer in essay form (with paragraphs, not single sentences or outline form). *Stop after 15 minutes.*

1. What was the procedure (method) of this study?
2. What factors were tested?
3. What were the conclusions of the study?

C

After you take the test, read the lecture (p. 94). Did you cover all the main points? If not, perhaps you did not use your time well during the test (spending too much time on a detail). On the other hand, perhaps something was missing from your notes.

31 • Lecture: Thought Group Markers

Take notes while listening to this lecture. Then compare your notes with the script (page 95). Did you miss any important points? Are your notes easy for you to read, so that you could use them to study for an examination?

Thought Group Markers 🔲

32 • Lecture: Techniques for Oral Presentation

Take notes while listening to this lecture. Then compare your notes with the script (page 97). Did you get the most important points? Can you use any of the suggestions in this lecture? Although the lecturer is talking about university presentations, these ideas are equally useful for business talks or any other kind of public speech.

Techniques for Oral Presentation

CLEAR SPEECH

33 · *Student's own dictation*

Dictation

1. Read aloud two long sentences from your own field of study and record them. Then write any technical terms that are unfamiliar to the class on the board.
2. Now dictate the sentences to the class.
3. Two or more fellow students should then write their versions of your dictation on the board. Missing words should be indicated by dashes or brackets. At the same time, you write your own version on the board.
4. With the help of the teacher, the class should now analyze the errors and misunderstandings.

Analysis

Compare the speaker version and the listener versions. Missing or faulty words may be a *listener* error. However, if two or more listeners misunderstood the same word, this is a sharp indication that you must correct some error in your speech.

1. *Identify the content words.* Content words (nouns, main verbs, etc.) are far more likely than structure words (articles, prepositions, etc.) to cause trouble with communication. For instance, a noun mistaken for a verb is certain to make it hard for the listener to predict what kinds of words are coming next.
2. *Circle the focus words.* A long sentence is apt to have several clauses, and each will have a focus (possibly two). A missed focus word will cause major confusion of the thought.
3. *Check the stressed syllables of focus words.* Was the stress on the right syllable? Were the sounds accurate? These are the critical syllables for clarity. A substitution of the wrong sound at these points is serious.
4. Can anyone in the class think of another possible source of error?

Conclusion

The class should practice the sentences with you, so that everybody understands and can apply the analysis. Now you should re-record the sentences. Together the class can compare the two versions on tape.

34 · Student's oral report

Each student will give a five-minute oral report on his or her field of interest, or other topic. This talk must not be read from a script, but delivered from outline notes.

The rest of the class should take notes on the talk. If possible, the talk should be taped for study at home or in the language laboratory.

The class and the teacher should then help the speaker analyze the clarity of the oral report, judging by the ease with which they could take notes from the talk. Consider the following points during your analysis:

1. *Amount of information.* Was there too much for a five-minute talk?
2. *Focus words.* Were they clearly pronounced?
3. *Thought groups.* Were they clearly marked?
4. *Technical terms (or especially important new information).* Were there adequate pauses afterward, to allow the listener to think about what was just heard?
5. *Organization.* Was it in logical sequence to help the listener predict what might come next?
6 DID THE SPEAKER MAKE IT EASY FOR THE LISTENER TO UNDERSTAND? That is the essence of clear speech.

35 · Problem sound contrasts: consonants

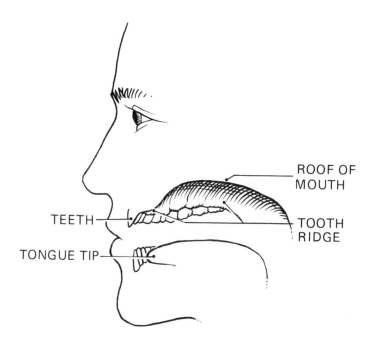

ROOF OF
MOUTH

TEETH

TOOTH
RIDGE

TONGUE TIP

r/l

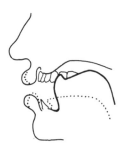 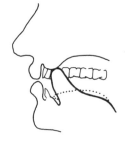

Two Steps to "r"

1. Say "ahhh"...(dotted line in figure)
2. Continue voicing, curl tongue tip back (solid line)

Notice the difference in the lips.

Two Steps to "l"

1. Say "ahhh"...(dotted line in figure)
2. Continue voicing, reach tip forward (solid line)

A

Practice these sounds slowly, until you can say them with a clear contrast.

1. ara, ala, ara, ala   aray, alay, aray, alay
   aree, alee, aree, alee   aro, alo, aro, alo
2. eera, eela   eeray, eelay   eeree, eelee   eero, eelo
3. arai, alai   aru, alu   ara, alee, aro, eelo
4. la, lay, lee, lo, lu   ra, ray, ree, ro, ru
5. ra, la, ray, lay, ree, ro, lo, ru, lu

B

Practice saying the following words with another student. Then ask "Which column?"

1	*2*	*3*
ray	lay	day
row	low	dough
reap	leap	deep
red	led	dead
room	loom	doom
rye	lie	die

C

Practice saying the following questions with another student. Answer according to which question you hear.

1a. Is it right?   No, it's wrong.
 b. Is it light?   No, it's dark.
2a. What's a lamb?   A baby sheep.
 b. What's a ram?   A male sheep.
3a. Where's the load?   In the truck.
 b. Where's the road?   Through the valley.

D

Practice saying this nonsense verse.

> I think that's not an alligator;
> it's not a crocodile.
> It won't go on the elevator,
> because the people smile.

v/b

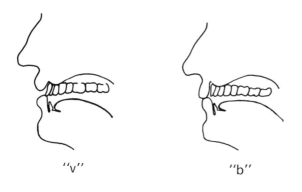

"v"   "b"

A

Practice saying these contrasts.

vet....bet
van....ban
very...berry
vase...base

B

Practice saying the following questions with another student and giving the correct responses.

1a. He wants to buy my boat.   Will you sell it?
 b. He wants to buy my vote.   That's against the law!
2a. What's a bat?   A kind of flying mouse.
 b. What's a vat?   A big container for liquid.

f/p

The continuant "f" is made like "v," but it is unvoiced. The stop "p" is made like "b," but it is unvoiced.

A

Practice saying these contrasts.

1   *2*

fat......pat
fail.....pail
fine.....pine
fool.....pool
foot....put
face.....pace

1   2

fast.....past
foal.....pole
feet.....Pete

B

Practice saying these questions and giving the correct answers.

1a. What does "fast" mean?   Quick.
 b. What does "past" mean?   Something is finished.
2a. What's a fool?   A stupid person.
 b. What's a pool?   A place to swim.
3a. What does "fine" mean?   Very good.
 b. What does "pine" mean?   A kind of tree.
4a. What does "fair" mean?   Something like *equal*.
 b. What does "pair" mean?   Two of the same kind.
 c. What does "pear" mean?   A kind of fruit.
5a. What's a foal?   A baby horse.
 b. What's a pole?   A long stick or rod.

th/t

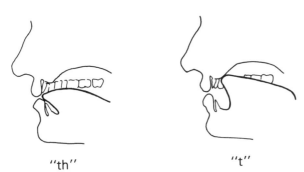

"th"   "t"

A

Practice the difference in saying these words.

	Continuants	Stops
Voiced	they.............	day
	than.............	Dan
	those............	doze
	loathe...........	load
Unvoiced	thought.........	taught
	thank...........	tank
	thin.............	tin
	theme..........	team
	bath.............	bat

B

Practice this limerick from page 65, this time concentrating on the clarity of the "th" and "t" sounds:

> The teachers are quick to suggest
> that we study quite hard for a test.
> It takes lots of thought
> to learn what we're taught.
> But I think I prefer just to rest.

th/s/z

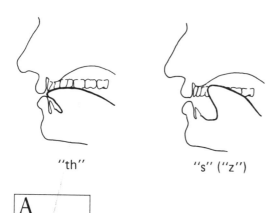

"th"   "s" ("z")

A

Practice the difference in saying these words. Take turns testing the class.

	1	*2*
Voiced	then.........Zen	
	thee.........."z"	
	clothe........close	
	clothing.....closing	
Unvoiced	thin.........sin	
	thought......sought	
	thank........sank	
	math.........mass	

B

Take turns testing the class with these questions.

1a. What's a path?   A small road for walkers.
 b. What's a pass?   An opening in the mountain (or a free ticket).
2a. What does "rising" mean?   Going up.
 b. What does "writhing" mean?   Twisting and turning (like a snake).

sh/ch

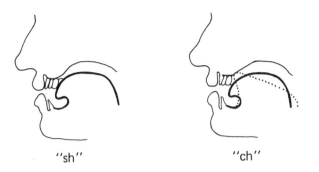

"sh"   "ch"

The "ch" sound is a combination of "t" (a stop) and then "sh" (a continuant). The contrast between "ch" and "sh" is a contrast between a combined stop-continuant and a simple continuant.

A

Practice the difference in saying these words.

1   *2*

share .....chair
shoe ......chew
sheep.....cheap
dish.......ditch
cash ......catch

B

Practice saying these questions and giving the correct answers. Take turns testing the class.

1a. Where's my share?   There isn't enough for everybody.
 b. Where's my chair?   In the other room.
2a. What are you washing?   The dishes.
 b. What are you watching?   The TV.

Self-analysis

Record the following words and then check for the clarity of the contrast between the stops and the continuants.

1. wife, wipe   both, boat
2. theme, team   day, they
3. I want to cash it. I want to catch it.

36 • Vowels

The diagrams below show the position of the tongue for three contrasting vowels.

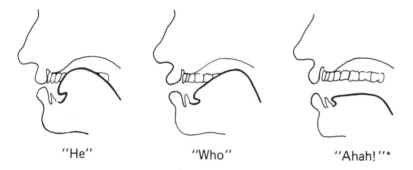

"He"   "Who"   "Ahah!"*

The diagram below shows the relationship between English vowels, according to the position of the highest point of the tongue.

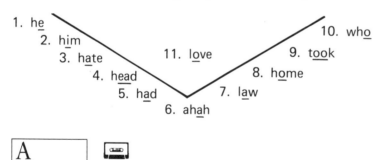

1. he
2. him
3. hate
4. head
5. had
6. ahah
7. law
8. home
9. took
10. who
11. love

A [cassette]

Listen to the contrast of vowel 11 and all the other vowels.

1. beat	11. but
2. bit	but
3. bait	but
4. bet	but
5. bat	but
6. bot	but
7. bought	but
8. boat	but
9. book	buck
10. boot	but

*"Ahah!" means "Now I understand!"

88

B 🔲 📼

Listen to the following repetitions of a word. One word is different in each set of words. Which word has vowel 11? (Which word is different?) Circle the number for that word.

Check your answers on p. 91. Practice the word sets that you got wrong.

1.	1	2	3	4	10.	1	2	3	4
2.	1	2	3	4	11.	1	2	3	4
3.	1	2	3	4	12.	1	2	3	4
4.	1	2	3	4	13.	1	2	3	4
5.	1	2	3	4	14.	1	2	3	4
6.	1	2	3	4	15.	1	2	3	4
7.	1	2	3	4	16.	1	2	3	4
8.	1	2	3	4	17.	1	2	3	4
9.	1	2	3	4	18.	1	2	3	4

C

Practice saying the following questions and giving the answers.

1a. Is it a big cat?   No, it's a dog.
 b. Is it a big cut?   No, not too deep.
2a. What's a "buck"?   One dollar.
 b. What's a book?   The thing you're reading.
3a. Was it cut?   No, it was broken.
 b. Was it caught?   No, it's still free.
4a. What's a skull?   The protection for your brain.
 b. What's a school?   A place for learning.
5a. Do you need many?   No, just a few.
 b. Do you need money?   Yes, $10.
6a. What's a goal?   An aim or purpose.
 b. What's a gull?   A sea bird.

D 🔲 📼

Vowels (h<u>e</u> and h<u>im</u>). Listen to the following repetitions of a word. One word is different in each set of words. Which one is different? Circle the number for that word. Check your answers on p. 91. Practice the word sets that you got wrong.

a.	1	2	3	4	e	1	2	3	4
b.	1	2	3	4	f.	1	2	3	4
c.	1	2	3	4	g.	1	2	3	4
d.	1	2	3	4	h.	1	2	3	4

E

Practice contrasting these columns of words.

he   *him*

feet ......fit
eat........it
seen .....sin
teen......tin
steal .....still
seat......sit

F

Practice saying these sounds pronouncing some of their possible spellings.

he   *him*

read   gift
teach   picnic
reach   nickle
bean   little
speak   Britain

needle   symbol
seem   syllable
keep   myth

thief
belief

G

Practice saying the following questions and their answers.

1a. Why did you sleep?   I was tired.
 b. Why did you slip?   The floor was wet.
2a. What's a sheep for?   Wool.
 b. What's a ship for?   To carry things on the water.
3a. When will you leave?   In two weeks.
 b. When will you live?   I'm living now.

   Practice vowel contrasts in these sentences:

4a. Is (h)e busy? (Izzybizzy?)
    Did (h)e visit the city?

Answers to B

	1	2	3	4
1.	bean	bean	bean	bun
2.	leave	leave	love	leave
3.	win	won	win	win
4.	hair	her	hair	hair
5.	stair	stair	stir	stair
6.	ran	ran	run	ran
7.	stunned	stand	stand	stand
8.	rob	rob	rob	rub
9.	hot	hot	hut	hot
10.	Don	done	Don	Don
11.	dock	duck	dock	dock
12.	wrong	wrong	rung	wrong
13.	gone	gun	gone	gone
14.	rum	roam	roam	roam
15.	room	rum	room	room
16.	sign	sign	sun	sign
17.	does	dies	dies	dies
18.	raced	rust	raced	raced

Answers to D

	1	2	3	4
a.	seek	seek	seek	sick
b.	feet	feet	fit	feet
c.	reach	rich	reach	reach
d.	still	steal	steal	steal
e.	teen	teen	tin	teen
f.	peach	pitch	peach	peach
g.	lick	leak	lick	lick
h.	bead	bid	bid	bid

Transcripts

Unit 25: Hearing numbers

```
A
```

Ingredients: one-half cup or a hundred thirteen grams white sugar
one-half cup or a hundred thirteen grams brown sugar
two-thirds cup or a hundred sixty-eight grams butter
one egg
one teaspoon or five milliliters vanilla
one and a half cups or two hundred fifteen grams flour
one-half teaspoon or two point five grams salt
one-half teaspoon or two point five grams baking soda
three-fourths cup or eighty-five grams nuts
six ounces or a hundred seventy grams chocolate chips

Method: Heat the oven to three hundred seventy-five degrees Fahrenheit or a hundred ninety degrees Celsius. Mix sugars, butter, egg, and vanilla thoroughly. Stir in remaining ingredients. Drop by rounded teaspoonfuls about two inches or five centimeters apart on ungreased cookie sheet. Bake eight to ten minutes until light brown. Cool slightly before removing from cookie sheet. This recipe makes about three and a half dozen cookies, which is forty-two individual cookies.

Unit 28: Age and Language Learning*

Most people think that the older you get, the harder it is to learn a new language. That is, they believe that children learn more easily and efficiently than adults. Thus, at some point in our lives, maybe around age 12 or 13, we lose the ability to learn languages well. Is this idea fact or myth?

Is it true that children learn a foreign language more efficiently than adults? On the contrary, research studies suggest that the opposite may be true. One report, on 2,000 Danish children studying Swedish, concluded that the teenagers learned more, in less time, than the younger children. Another report, on Americans learning Russian, showed a direct improvement of ability over

---

*Adapted from Evelyn Hatch, "Optimal age or optimal learners?," *Workpapers in Teaching English as a Second Language*, Vol. X (1977): 45–56, and from Stephen Krashen, Michael Long, and Robin Scarcella, "Age, rate, and eventual attainment in second language acquisition," *TESOL Quarterly*, Vol. 13 (1979): 573–582.

the age range tested; that is, the ability to learn increased as the age increased, from childhood to adulthood.

There are several possible explanations for these findings. For one thing, adults know more about the world and therefore are able to understand meanings more easily than children. Moreover, adults can use logical thinking to help themselves see patterns in the language. Finally, adults have more self-discipline than children.

All in all, it seems that the common idea that children are better language learners than adults may not be fact, but myth.

Unit 29: Guides to Universities

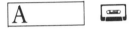

Do you intend to study at an American university? It takes a long time to get accepted at most American schools, perhaps as much as a year. That's why you should start choosing a school as soon as possible. It's also a good idea to apply to several different institutions, so that you'll have a better chance of acceptance at one. You should start looking for information now, because the more information you have about each college, the better choice you can make.

There are two good ways to get the information you need. One is a general reference book, called *Guide to American Colleges and Universities*. The other good source of information is the catalogue published by each school.

You can study the general guide in almost any American library. This book has many useful statistics, such as the number of students, the average test scores for people accepted to the school, the number of books in the library, and the number of faculty members. You can also find the address of each school in this book.

Although the general guidebook has helpful information, some of the facts may be out-of-date. For instance, many schools raise their tuition every year. Since you'll need to know what your education will cost, out-of-date information will not be good enough. Also, schools sometimes change their requirements for entrance. To be sure that you are getting current information, write to the university and ask for its catalogue.

The catalogue not only has more current facts than the guidebook, but it also has more detailed information. For instance, the catalogue can tell you if there is a special foreign student adviser, what kind of courses are offered, and what kind of housing is available. Some universities have dormitories, but at others you have to find your own place to live.

With all of this information, you should be able to pick out several good schools.

B

Questions. Stop the tape after each question.

1. What was the main topic of this talk?
2. What can you find in a general guide to universities?

3. According to the speaker, what is one reason you should write for a catalogue?
4. What is tuition?
5. What does the word "housing" mean?

Unit 30: Pronunciation Achievement Factors

We all know that it is difficult for adults to learn accurate pronunciation in a foreign language. We also know that some people achieve better results than others. Why is this? What are the factors that might predict which students will achieve good pronunciation? If we knew the factors helping pronunciation, we could improve our own learning.

Richard Suter, a language researcher at a California university, decided to test the relative importance of factors that might predict which students would achieve the most accurate pronunciation.* He wanted to find out if there are any factors a student could change in order to improve performance.

The first thing Suter did was to make a list of all the factors that might possibly show which students would learn the best pronunciation. Then he compared these factors with the pronunciation of a group of foreign students. Here is a list of six of the factors that Suter studied.

1. Sex. Do females learn better than males?
2. Mother tongue. Is it easier to learn a language close to one's own?
3. Personality. Do out-going people learn pronunciation better than shy people?
4. Attitude toward pronunciation. Does it make a difference if the student believes that pronunciation is a very important part of language?
5. Natural ability. How important is the ability to mimic, or imitate? Most people assume that natural ability is the single most important factor in learning pronunciation.
6. Conversation with natives. Does the amount of conversation in English, with native speakers of English, make a significant difference?

When Suter compared the students' pronunciation accuracy scores with these six variables, some of the results were surprising. He found that two of the factors did not have *any* relation to the accuracy of pronunciation. That is, these two factors were not at all significant in predicting who would do well learning pronunciation. These two factors were:

1. Sex. Females were not better than males.
2. Personality. Out-going people were not better at pronunciation than shy people.

Suter concluded from these results that the factors of sex and personality were not significant predictors of pronunciation accuracy. On the other hand, he found that four variables did make a significant difference. I will give them to you in order of importance. That is, the most important predictors come first.

*R. Suter, "Predictors of pronunciation accuracy in second language learning," *Language Learning*, Vol. 26, No. 2. (1976): 233–253.

1. Mother tongue. This was the most significant factor in predicting achievement. If the student's own language was closer to English, the achievement was likely to be greater.
2. Attitude about pronunciation. This was the second most important factor in predicting achievement. In fact, a belief in the importance of pronunciation was far more important than any of the remaining factors. After the mother tongue factor, this factor of attitude was the single most significant variable in predicting good pronunciation learning.
3. Conversation with natives. The third most important variable was the amount of time the student spent in conversation with native speakers of English.
4. Natural ability. This was the least important variable. The ability to imitate helped, but it was not nearly as significant as most people think. It was far less significant than the first three.

Suter concluded that the three most significant predictors in achievement in pronunciation are: (1) the student's mother tongue, (2) the belief in the importance of pronunciation, and (3) the amount of time spent in conversations with native speakers.

The conclusions of this research are encouraging. Of course, we can't change factor 1, our mother tongue. But we *do* have control over factors 2 and 3, which are the next most important variables in learning accurate pronunciation. First, we can decide that pronunciation is important, and second, we can choose to make the effort to speak the new language with natives. You might say that our own choice is the most significant factor in achievement in the new language.

Unit 31: Thought Group Markers

Today I want to tell you about some useful research on the way English speakers help their listeners. You know that a lot of English sentences are very complicated. The listener can get confused if the thought groups aren't clearly divided. If the groups aren't clear, the ideas won't be clear. Each language has special ways to mark thought groups, but in English the chief marker is intonation. A researcher named O'Malley* thought of a clever way to study these markers. He knew that algebra problems have to be written with parentheses. These punctuation markers are used to group the terms. If the algebra is spoken out loud, a native speaker of English can hear the grouping. Let me give you an example. Write down this equation:

$$A + (B \times C) = Y$$

Now write down another one:

$$(A + B) \times C = Y$$

Did you write them differently? You should have put the parentheses in different places, because these equations are different.

---

*M. O'Malley, D. Kloker, and B. Dara-Abrams, "Recovering parentheses from spoken algebraic expressions," *IEEE Transactions on Audio and Electro-Acoustics*, AU-21 (1973): 217–220.

Perhaps you can get the idea better if I use examples from arithmetic. Write down this problem:

$$2 + (3 \times 4) = 14$$

Now write:

$$(2 + 3) \times 4 = 20$$

Did you put the parentheses in different places? The terms are exactly the same, but the grouping is different. That is why the answers are different.

The same concept of grouping also applies to words. Here's an example:

"John," said the boss, "is stupid."

That has a very different meaning from this sentence, using the same words:

John said, "The boss is stupid."

The meaning is different, just as in algebra or arithmetic. So grouping is important. Of course, speaking isn't like writing. We don't use parentheses or other punctuation when we're speaking. In fact, punctuation was invented to try to show some of the things we do in speech to separate groups of words. Written language substitutes punctuation for the spoken signals of intonation. The English listener depends on these intonation signals in order to understand clearly.

In his research on the subject of thought-group markers, O'Malley tape recorded native English speakers reading algebraic equations aloud. Then he asked some other English speakers to listen to the recordings and decide where the parentheses were placed. O'Malley found that both the speakers and the listeners were very consistent in grouping the terms. The listeners were able to identify the placement of the parentheses because the speakers used two markers to show the end of a group.

The first marker was *silence*. That is, the speaker paused after the group, to make clear that it was finished. Listen for the pause when I read this equation:

$$A \ldots + (B \times C) \ldots = Y$$

Marker 1, a pause, is quite powerful in slow speech. But in more rapid speech, there isn't time for many pauses. So the speaker has to rely on another method to mark the end of a group. Marker 2 is a change of pitch. Usually the voice pitch drops low at the end of a group. Generally, a high pitch means a new idea, and a low pitch means the end of an idea. Listen for the pitch change when I read this equation.

$$(A + B) \times C = Y$$

Other researchers* have confirmed these findings for spoken English. In both algebraic formulas and spoken English, the thought groups are divided by the same two markers. With Marker 1, which is especially used for slow

*D. Klatt, "Vowel lengthening is syntactically determined in connected discourse," *Journal of Phonetics*, Vol. 3 (1975): 139; Ilse Lehiste, "Isochrony reconsidered," *Journal of Phonetics*, Vol. 5, (1977): 253–263.

speech, the speaker pauses at the end of each group. With Marker 2, the voice falls at the end of a group. For special clarity, both markers are used.

I've reviewed some of this research because it shows a very important way to help our listeners understand us easily. It demonstrates the ways of making thought groups clear. Clear thought groups are part of clear speech.

Unit 32: Techniques for Oral Presentation

In your university work, you will be expected to give oral presentations, in the form of reports or simply in the form of answers to questions. There are several things you can do to make your oral presentations clear and easy to understand.

The essential point to realize is that speech and writing are different. If you want to be clearly understood, you can't simply read your written report aloud. The biggest difference between spoken and written language is that readers can look back over the printed words when they don't understand. In spoken language, however, listeners can't go back and check the words. They can rely only on memory. So the first principle to keep in mind when you're planning to speak in public is that you have to help the listener's memory. This means that an oral report can't deliver information as rapidly as a written report. That is, you can't have as many pieces of new information packed into the same number of words, because they will come at too fast a rate for the listener to understand.

In an oral report, the rate of delivery has to be slower. One of the best ways to help your audience is simply to speak slowly. Many people speak too fast when they speak to a group. This is a mistake, especially if you have a foreign accent, because it makes listening more difficult. Beyond the simple technique of speaking more slowly when you speak before a group, there are ways of organizing your presentation that can help the listener recognize and understand your main points.

The organization of your talk should allow enough time for the listener to think both *before* and *after* each new idea. The purpose of the time before the new information is to give the audience a chance to understand the background clearly. Knowledge of the background, or setting of the information, makes it much easier to anticipate what kind of information is coming next. If the new information occurs too early, without enough background, the listener isn't prepared to understand the new idea. So before each piece of information, the listeners should be prepared with enough background to be able to predict what's coming.

I've been describing the time for thinking *before* the new information. It's also important to provide time for thinking *after* the new information. This thinking time allows listeners to fit the idea into their general knowledge of the subject. Thinking time gives the listener a chance to make sure the idea was understood before going on to the next new idea.

There are three common ways to give the listener time for thinking after a point of new information. One way is simply to pause. A moment of silence gives the listener time to take in the new information, but there are other ways. A second method is to use a paraphrase. That is, you say the same thing, but in different words. This paraphrase, or repetition of the idea, helps the listeners to fix the thought in their memory. A third way to give the listener time to think is to use words that don't mean much. These are words that convey no information, but just fill time. For instance, you might say something like "as I've been saying" or "and so forth and so on." That kind of expression doesn't really say anything. It's just made of what we call "filler words." The words have no real meaning, but they do perform a useful function, since they allow the listener time to think.

In summary, then, we know that oral language should deliver information at a slower rate than you can use in written language. New information should be presented more gradually. Thinking time should be provided both before and after each important new item. The time *before* is to provide a background so that the listeners can have a chance to anticipate the idea. The time *after* is to allow the listeners a chance to understand what they just heard. The three most common ways to allow this thinking time are: (1) to pause, (2) to paraphrase, and (3) to use filler words.

I hope that these suggestions will help make your oral presentations a great success.